Central Arizona Trail Information

#	Trail Name	FS#	Length	Elev.	Change
1	La Barge Creek - Boulder Canyon	#103			
2	Upper Fish Creek Canyon	-			
3	Lower Fish Creek Canyon	-			
4	Workman Creek - The Tubs	-			
5	Workman Creek - The Forest	-			
6	Reynolds Creek - Hells Hole	#148	6.0 miles	5200'	1500'
7	Reynolds Creek - The Falls	#150	1 - 4 miles	6160'	300' - 1040'
8	Aravaipa Canyon	-	4 - 11 miles	2600'	200' - 440'
9	Little Saddle Mountain	#244	2 - 5 miles	3720'	600' - 1280'
10	Deer Creek	#43	2 - 10 miles	3360'	200' - 2240'
11	Barnhart	#45	3 - 6 miles	4200'	1600' - 1920'
12	Tonto Creek - Indian Farm	-	3.0 miles	2840'	160'
13	Tonto Creek - Bear Flat Campground	-	1.5 miles	4960'	100'
14	Christopher Creek - Box Canyon	#298	0.6 miles	5680'	280'
15	Hunter Creek	-	2.5 miles	6160'	60'
16	Gordon Creek	-	1 - 3 miles	6260'	50' - 100'
17	Horton Creek	#285	3.8 miles	5480'	980'
18	Christopher Creek - See Canyon	#184	4.7 miles	5820'	2060'
19	Canyon Creek	-	5.0 miles	6500'	260'
20	Willow Springs Lake	-	3.5 miles	7510'	60'
21	Woods Canyon Lake	-	4.5 miles	7500'	60'
22	East Chevelon Creek	-	2.0 miles	7460'	100'
23	Bear Canyon Lake	-	2.0 miles	7560'	100'
24	East Verde River - Water Wheel CG	-	0.3 miles	4960'	40'
25	Ellison Creek	-	1.5 miles	5200'	160'
26	East Verde River - Flowing Springs CG	-	0.8 miles	4460'	40'
27	East Webber Creek	#289	3.8 miles	5400'	960'
28	Pine Canyon	#26	4 - 7 miles	7240'	1440' - 1840'
29	Fossil Springs	#98	2.5 miles	5600'	1320'
30	Fossil Creek Bridge	-	0.2 miles	3600'	80'
31	Verde River - Verde Hot Springs	-	0.7 miles	2640'	160'
32	Verde River - Needle Rock	-	1 - 4 miles	1560'	160' - 500'
33	Cave Creek	#4	3 - 10 miles	3400'	400' - 1200'
34	Verde River - Sheep's Bridge	#11	2 - 8 miles	2060'	340' - 580'
35	Sycamore Creek - Parson Springs	#144	2 - 4 miles	3600'	200' - 300'
36	West Clear Creek	#17	3 - 6 miles	3600'	200' - 2400'
37	Rarick Canyon	-	1 - 2 miles	3920'	60' - 110'
38	Wet Beaver Creek - Bell	#13	3 - 9 miles	3880'	60' - 1800'
39	Oak Creek - Allen's Bend	#111	0.8 miles	4400'	80'
40	Oak Creek - Slide Rock	-	0.5 miles	4920'	60'
41	West Fork of Oak Creek	#108	3 - 13 miles	5280'	200' - 800'
42	Dry Beaver Creek - Woods Canyon	#93	3.0 miles	3840'	500'
43	Oak Creek - Red Rock Crossing	-	0.5 miles	3960'	20'
44	Oak Creek - Kisva	-	1.5 miles	3880'	160'
45	Watson Lake	-	0.5 miles	5160'	40'
46	Goldwater Lake	-	1.2 miles	6000'	60'
47	Lynx Lake - Lake Shore Trail	-	2.5 miles	5480'	60'
48	Hassayampa Lake	-	0.8 miles	6680'	40'
49	Hassayampa Preserve River Trail	-	1.5 miles	1980'	50'
50	Burro Creek	-	1.5 miles	1920'	40'

Published in the United States by Pinyon Publishing Company
P.O. Box 23809, Tempe, Arizona 85285-3809

Photographs and Maps by Steve Krause
Printed by Arrowhead Press, Phoenix, Arizona

Acknowledgements

Thanks are given to the National Forest Service for their helpfulness, guidance, and concern in my hiking endeavors. Special appreciation is expressed to family and friends who have shared the outdoor experiences -- Betty, Elmer, Don, Linda, Kelly, Andy, Matt, Dan,Veena, Vichai, Mimi, Boy, Charlie, Doug, Don, Rosemary, John, Carol, Wade, Mert, Peter, and Doris.

ISBN # 0-910973-09-1

Liability Waiver

Due to the possibility of personal error, typographical error, misinterpretation of information, and the many changes both natural and man made, the author and publisher and all other persons or companies directly artd indirectly associated with this publication assume no responsibility for accidents, injury, damage, or losses by individuals or groups using this publication. In rough terrain and hazardous areas all persons are advised to be aware of possible changes due to the elements or those hazards which may be man made that can occur along any of the trails.

STREAMSIDE TRAILS:

Day Hiking Central Arizona's Lakes, Rivers, and Creeks

Steve Krause

Christopher Creek flows through the chiseled basalt blocks of Box Canyon

Contents

Chapter 1. How to Use This Book   8

Chapter 2. Central Arizona Overview   10

Waters of Central Arizona   10
Accessing Central Arizona   12
Day Hiking the Seasons   14

Chapter 3. Central Arizona Trails   16

Choosing a Hike   16
   Easier Trails   18
   Moderate Trails   20
   More Challenging Trails   22
   Waterfall and Swimming Hole Trails   24
Hiking Preparations   26
Hiking Precautions   27
Environmental Courtesy   28
Agency Information   29

Chapter 4. East Central Arizona Trails   30

Area I. Apache Junction Vicinity   32

1 - LaBarge Creek - Boulder Canyon Trail FS#103   34
2 - Fish Creek - Upper Canyon Trail   36
3 - Fish Creek - Lower Canyon Trail   38

Area II. Globe Vicinity   40

4 - Workman Creek - The Tubs Trail   42
5 - Workman Creek - Forest Trail   44
6 - Reynolds Creek - Hells Hole Trail FS#148   46
7 - Reynolds Creek - The Falls Trail FS#150   48
8 - Aravaipa Canyon Trail   50

Ch. 5. Northeast Central Arizona Trails   52

Area III. Payson South Vicinity   54

9 - Little Saddle Mountain Trail FS#244   56
10 - Deer Creek Trail FS#45   58
11 - Barnhart Trail FS#43   60
12 - Tonto Creek - Indian Farm Trail   62

Area IV. Payson East Vicinity   64

13 - Tonto Creek - Bear Flat Campground Trail   66
14 - Christopher Creek - Box Canyon Trail FS#298   68
15 - Hunter Creek Trail   70
16 - Gordon Creek Trail   72
17 - Horton Creek Trail FS#285   74
18 - Christopher Creek - See Canyon Trail FS#184   76
19 - Canyon Creek Trail   78
20 - Willow Springs Lake Trail   80
21 - Woods Canyon Lake Trail   82
22 - East Chevelon Creek Trail   84
23 - Bear Canyon Lake Trail   86

Area V. Payson West Vicinity   88

24 - East Verde River - Water Wheel CG Trail   90
25 - Ellison Creek Trail   92
26 - East Verde River - Flowing Springs CG Trail   94
27 - East Webber Creek Trail FS#289   96
28 - Pine Canyon Trail FS#26   98
29 - Fossil Springs Trail FS#98   100
30 - Fossil Creek - Bridge Trail   102
31 - Verde River - Verde Hot Springs Trail   104

Chapter 6. North Central Arizona Trails 106

Area VI. Carefree Vicinity 108

3 2 - Verde River - Needle Rock Trail 110
3 3 - Cave Creek Trail FS#4 112
3 4 - Verde River at Sheep Bridge Trail FS#11 114

Area VII. Camp Verde Vicinity 116

3 5 - Sycamore Creek - Parson Springs Trail FS#144 118
3 6 - West Clear Creek Trail FS#17 120
3 7 - Rarick Canyon Trail 122
3 8 - Wet Beaver Creek - Bell Trail FS#13 124

Area VIII. Sedona Vicinity 126

3 9 - Oak Creek - Allen's Bend Trail FS#111 128
4 0 - Oak Creek - Slide Rock State Park - Creek Trail 130
4 1 - West Fork Oak Creek Trail FS#108 132
4 2 - Dry Beaver Creek - Woods Canyon Trail FS#93 134
4 3 - Oak Creek - Red Rock Crossing Trail 136
4 4 - Oak Creek - Red Rock State Park - Kisva Trail 138

Ch. 7. Northwest Central Arizona Trails 140

Area IX. Prescott Vicinity 142

4 5 - Watson Lake Trail 144
4 6 - Goldwater Lake Trail 146
4 7 - Lynx Lake Trail 148
4 8 - Hassayampa Lake Trail 150

Area X. Wickenburg Vicinity 152

4 9 - Hassayampa Preserve River Trail 154
5 0 - Burro Creek Trail 156

Bibliography 158

Index 159

Chapter 1. How to Use This Book

You've walked next to bubbling waters and under the pines and maples on the lush and scenic West Fork Trail in Oak Creek Canyon - or maybe beneath the canopy of cottonwoods and sycamores while wading through the cool, clear, refreshing waters of Aravaipa Creek. The rich vegetation and dynamic wildlife always add an extra dimension to a streamside trail. But you live in the desert, and how many trails could there be with that extra dimension? There's plenty! Here's a summary of how to plan your riparian hikes with *Streamside Trails*.

Activity Planning

* **FIRST**, choose the exertion level and location of the hike from the lists shown in Chapter 3 - Easier, Moderate, Challenging, or Waterfall & Swimming Hole Trails

* **SECOND**, read the one-page "snapshot" description in these Central Arizona regions

    Chapter 4 - East Central - I. Apache Junction, **II.** Globe

    Chapter 5 - Northeast Central - III. Payson S, **IV.** Payson E, **V.** Payson W

    Chapter 6 - North Central - VI. Carefree, **VII.** Camp Verde, **VIII.** Sedona

    Chapter 7 - Northwest Central - IX. Prescott, **X.** Wickenburg

* **THIRD**, read directions from the "snapshot" description, use the finder and detail maps on the adjoining page, and use the regional map at the beginning of that chapter.

Understanding Central Arizona

If you have the time, read a bit of information on the geography, road access, and weather of Central Arizona in Chapter 2. You'll find out more about the history of each region in the stories in individual hike "snapshot" descriptions.

Rock hopping (jump and pray) is a skill often used on streamside hikes.

"Snapshot" Activity Descriptions

There are 50 one-page descriptions of streamside trails with maps on the adjoining page that show the trail location and the trail itself.

Each "snapshot" description includes:

1) the title of the hiking trail which has:
    a) a ``Streamside Trail'' hike number (underlined), and
    b) an optional Forest Service number (FS#) for maintained hiking trails.

2) summary details of information about a hiking trail that include:
    a) distance - refers to the one-way distance along a hiking trail
    b) elevation change - refers to the one-way elevation gain (or loss)
    c) elevation - affects temperature; if it's 90° at 4000' it will be about 78° at 7000'
    d) seasons (preferred) - some locations may be closed or trails may be too hot or cold
    e) agency - who to contact for info, eg. National Forest (NF), Ranger District (RD)
    f) topos - refers to the United States Geological Survey 7.5° topographic maps

3) paragraphs with a frontier history "nugget" and with directions and highlights of the hike

4) specific directions for finding a Forest Service trailhead or trail access for primitive trails

5) a photo taken at the trailhead or along the hiking trail.

Day Hiking Tips

* **Selection** - Choose the type of experience you want and plan the route. Avoid the most popular trails on summer weekends or arrive early so you'll find a place to park.
* **Access** - To check if a trail is open call the Forest Service or other appropriate agency for current information on area weather and trail access and condition.
* **Hiking Experience** - If you're inexperienced, or haven't hiked the area before, read the sections in Chapter 3 on Hike Planning, Preparations, and Precautions.

Glossary of Terms and Abbreviations

BLM - Bureau of Land Management

Can - Canyon

CG - Campground

Crk - Creek

flume - chute or tube which carries water

Hwy - Highway

FR#100 - Forest Service Road #100

FS#200 - Forest Service Trail #200

MP#100 - Milepost Marker #100

Mtn - Mountain

NF - National Forest

NM - National Monument

Pk - Peak

RD - Ranger District

Rim - the Mogollon Rim

riparian - of a streamside environment

TH - Trailhead

topos - topographic maps

travertine - formed by spring deposition

Vly - Valley

Central Arizona Creeks & Rivers

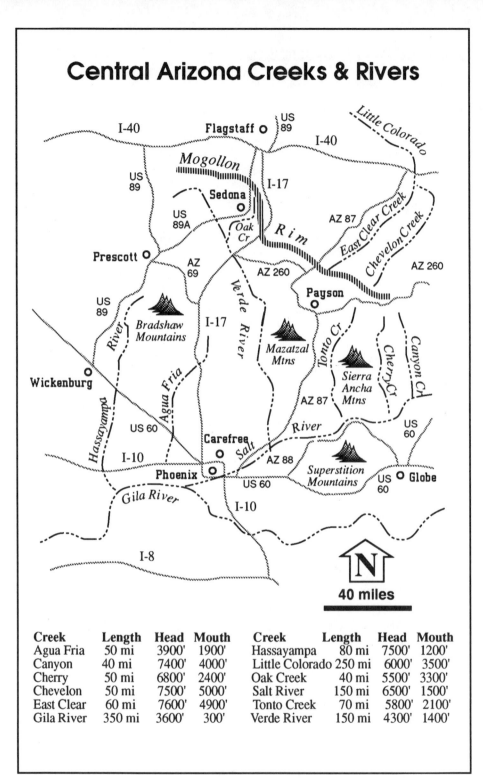

Creek	Length	Head	Mouth	Creek	Length	Head	Mouth
Agua Fria	50 mi	3900'	1900'	Hassayampa	80 mi	7500'	1200'
Canyon	40 mi	7400'	4000'	Little Colorado	250 mi	6000'	3500'
Cherry	50 mi	6800'	2400'	Oak Creek	40 mi	5500'	3300'
Chevelon	50 mi	7500'	5000'	Salt River	150 mi	6500'	1500'
East Clear	60 mi	7600'	4900'	Tonto Creek	70 mi	5800'	2100'
Gila River	350 mi	3600'	300'	Verde River	150 mi	4300'	1400'

Ch. 2. Central Arizona Overview
Waters of Central Arizona

Arizona is a desert, but a desert interwoven with streams that run down towering mountain ranges and across long plateaus. Water adds another dimension to the outdoor experience when hiking around a lake, beside a river, or through a creek. Mostly everyone has a favorite streamside hike or two. There's the soaring canyon walls of West Fork Creek near Sedona, the almost alpine forest of Lynx Lake by Prescott, and the stunning fall colors of Deer Creek south of Payson. But there's a lot more. This book offers new opportunities to access 50 trails by lakes, rivers, and creeks within a few hours of Phoenix.

The geologic transformations of time have graced Central Arizona with outcropped mountains and grooved plains where fresh streams run through hundreds of canyons. In the middle of the uplifted Colorado Plateau, erosion by the Colorado River carved the deep and majestic Grand Canyon. The southern border of this plateau, which drops steeply and traces a 150 mile line across the middle of the state, is known as the Mogollon Rim. The eastern half of the Rim runs southeast from Payson, and has canyon streams which flow southward into Tonto Creek which, in turn, empties into the Salt River at Roosevelt Lake. The western half of the Rim moves northward, skirting Camp Verde, and then westward, sliding past Sedona. Its streams run into the Verde, which also drains into the Salt River near Phoenix.

South of the Mogollon Rim are volcanic mountain ranges that are patches of corrugated earth jutting from the desert plain. They lie on a trace that circles Phoenix from east to north to west. The parched and hostile Superstition Mountain range lies east of Apache Junction and has winter creeks that drain into the Salt River. The jagged Sierra Anchas lie to the northwest of Globe and have cliffs that have struck high waterfalls, charging streams with waters that also run to the Salt River. The woody eastern half of the Mazatzals lies south of Payson and drains into the Tonto. The western half of the Mazatzals, which are accessed north of Carefree, drain westward into the Verde. The rugged northern Bradshaw Mountains lie south of Prescott and drain north into the Verde, whereas the southern Bradshaws lie north of Wickenburg and drain south into the Hassayampa River which then runs to the Gila.

So it is that the overall area below the eastern Mogollon Rim drains into the Salt River, while the area below the western Rim drains into the Verde River, which then drains into the Salt. Finally, all waters of the Salt flow into the Gila River. In reality, however, it is only the broad, parched bed of the Salt River that intersects the wide, dusty, dry bed of the Gila River.

Ultimately, the Colorado River captures any moisture from Central Arizona still left after seepage, evaporation, impoundment, or consumption. The Colorado runs across the northern boundary of the state of Arizona and receives any water that the Little Colorado has collected from creeks on top of the Mogollon Rim. At the northwest corner of Arizona the Colorado turns south and defines most of the western boundary of the state. It also collects the waters of the Gila River which have been fed by the creeks running southward from the lower edge of the Mogollon Rim. But it is curiously unfortunate that both the Little Colorado and the Gila usually run dry before reaching the Colorado River.

The land of Central Arizona, which spans an area of about 100 by 200 miles, collects an average rainfall of 10" to 20" per year, or 500 billion gallons of water per year. Yet, for most of the year, and sometimes all of it, there is no flow of this water into the Colorado. The reason is that the water removed from the state's creeks and rivers have left only 10% of their total length still free flowing. If you enjoy streamside hikes, do something to ensure that your favorite streams and trails are still here a century from now. Join and support a conservation organization - the Sierra Club, the American Rivers Society, the Nature Conservancy, or any of many other groups striving to preserve the remaining heritage for future generations.

Accessing Central Arizona

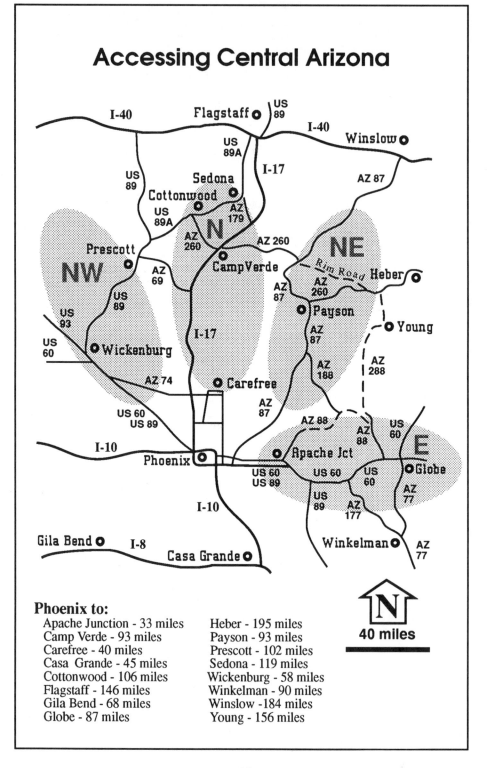

Phoenix to:

Apache Junction - 33 miles	Heber - 195 miles
Camp Verde - 93 miles	Payson - 93 miles
Carefree - 40 miles	Prescott - 102 miles
Casa Grande - 45 miles	Sedona - 119 miles
Cottonwood - 106 miles	Wickenburg - 58 miles
Flagstaff - 146 miles	Winkelman - 90 miles
Gila Bend - 68 miles	Winslow -184 miles
Globe - 87 miles	Young - 156 miles

Accessing Central Arizona

To simplify access to the streamside trails, their locations in Central Arizona have been divided into four general regions that fan out from four highways emanating from central Phoenix. Hiking trails that are close to one another have been grouped into areas which are in the vicinity of a town. In each of the four regions, there are then two or more areas that are in the vicinity of each of these towns.

East Central Arizona can be accessed by highway US 60. Traveling eastward about 30 miles from Phoenix is *Area I. Apache Junction Vicinity*. From there AZ 88, the scenic Apache Trail, branches off into the Superstition Wilderness that has winter trails along streams like Fish Creek or La Barge Creek. Further along US 60, 90 miles east of Phoenix, lies *Area II. Globe Vicinity*. Traveling northwest of Globe (20 miles on AZ 88 plus 25 miles on the washboard of AZ 288, Globe-Young Highway) will bring you to the Sierra Ancha Wilderness with fine waterfalls along trails such as Workman Creek and Reynolds Creek. Heading southeast of Globe on AZ 77 will access the fabled waters of Aravaipa Creek.

Northeast Central Arizona is accessed by highway AZ 87, Beeline Highway, by going 90 miles northeast to Payson. Streamside trails around Payson are so numerous that the region has been further subdivided into three areas available along the three routes emanating from the center of the town. Going south on AZ 87 goes to *Area III. South Payson Vicinity*, which includes the northern Mazatzal Wilderness, with spring time creek trails like Deer Creek and Barnhart Canyon. *Area IV. East Payson Vicinity* runs eastward on AZ 260 up to 40 miles along the Mogollon Rim. Below the Rim are scenic trails like Horton Creek and Canyon Creek. On the top of the Rim, which is reached by doubling back on the Rim Road (FS Road #300), there are the Rim Lakes with easy trails at locations like Woods Canyon Lake and Bear Canyon Lake. *Area V. West Payson Vicinity* runs northwest on AZ 87 along the lower edge of the Mogollon Rim with cool, forested trails like the East Webber Creek or Pine Creek Trails. Further ahead on AZ 87, a jog to the southwest on to Fossil Springs Road (FS Rd#708) will bring you to trails at the bottom of the Rim which have unique destinations, such as the Fossil Springs Trail and the Verde Hot Springs Trail.

North Central Arizona is generally accessed by I-17, Black Canyon Highway. Close to Phoenix is *Area VI. Carefree Vicinity*, east of I-17 about 10 miles. This is the jump off point for further travel on Cave Creek Road, FS#24, which accesses trails north of Carefree at Seven Springs and by the Verde River near the edge of the western Mazatzals. Further north on I-17 is Area *VII. Camp Verde Vicinity*. From there, going east or west on AZ 260, General Crook Highway, will lead to more trails from the edge of the western Mogollon Rim, such as Wet Beaver Creek or West Clear Creek. Further north on I-17 is the exit for *Area VIII. Sedona Vicinity*, which lies 15 miles north on AZ 179. From Sedona, there are trails south on AZ 179 like Woods Canyon. There are also more populated trails north on US 89A along Oak Creek Canyon like West Fork or Allens Bend, or west on US 89A near West Sedona, like Red Rock Crossing or the Kisva Trail at Red Rock State Park.

Northwest Central Arizona may be accessed either by traveling 60 miles north on I-17 and then 40 miles northwest on AZ 69 for *Area IX. Prescott Vicinity*, or by going northwest 60 miles on US 60 to *Area X.Wickenburg Vicinity*. From Prescott, going south into the Bradshaw Mountains on Senator Highway or on Walker Road, you'll find cool, forested trails around three lakes, Lynx, Goldwater, and Hassayampa. Going north of Prescott will access the the scenic, but warm, Watson Lake and Granite Dells. By Wickenburg, south of the Bradshaws, are nice desert riparian trails including the Hassayampa Preserve River Trail just southeast of town, and, to the northwest, the flat, broad, and rocky creek bed of the Burro Creek Trail.

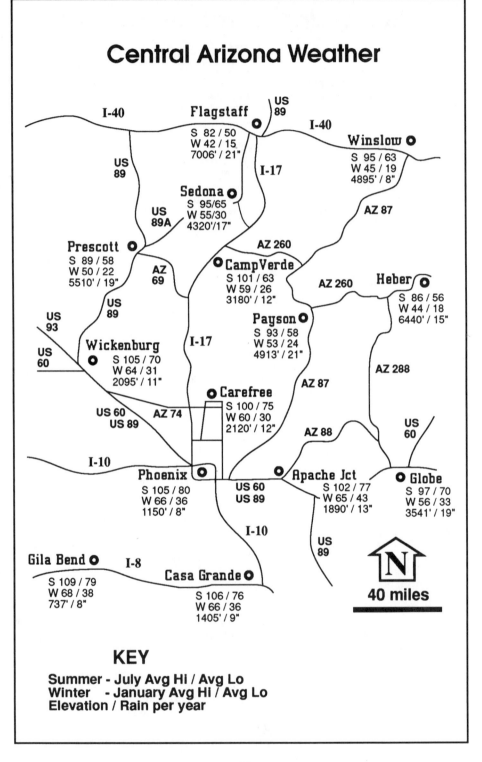

Central Arizona Weather

Flagstaff
S 82 / 50
W 42 / 15
7006' / 21"

I-40

US 89

US 89

I-17

Winslow
S 95 / 63
W 45 / 19
4895' / 8"

AZ 87

Sedona
S 95/65
W 55/30
4320'/17"

US 89A

Prescott
S 89 / 58
W 50 / 22
5510' / 19"

AZ 69

AZ 260

CampVerde
S 101 / 63
W 59 / 26
3180' / 12"

AZ 260

Heber
S 86 / 56
W 44 / 18
6440' / 15"

US 89

US 93

US 60

Payson
S 93 / 58
W 53 / 24
4913' / 21"

Wickenburg
S 105 / 70
W 64 / 31
2095' / 11"

I-17

AZ 288

AZ 87

Carefree
S 100 / 75
W 60 / 30
2120' / 12"

US 60
US 89

AZ 74

AZ 88

US 60

I-10

Phoenix
S 105 / 80
W 66 / 36
1150' / 8"

US 60
US 89

Apache Jct
S 102 / 77
W 65 / 43
1890' / 13"

Globe
S 97 / 70
W 56 / 33
3541' / 19"

I-10

US 89

N

40 miles

Gila Bend
I-8
S 109 / 79
W 68 / 38
737' / 8"

Casa Grande
S 106 / 76
W 66 / 36
1405' / 9"

KEY

Summer - July Avg Hi / Avg Lo
Winter - January Avg Hi / Avg Lo
Elevation / Rain per year

Day Hiking the Seasons

Each season brings moisture in its own way and so nurtures vegetation, wildlife, and the enjoyment of the day hiker. Winter storms build snowpack on the mountains and water low lying desert washes. Spring snow melt fills dry canyons and recharges perennial springs. Summer's violent "monsoon" thunderstorms quench a parched desert and can trigger flash floods. Fall dryness signals the end of another growing season and is punctuated only by an infrequent storm that puts a final bloom on flowered mountain meadows.

Does any other region in the world compare with Arizona for the variety of trails available for hiking year 'round? Decide for yourself. The personal comfort zone from 55F to 85F can always be found somewhere in Central Arizona, as can be seen on the Weather Map. That's because increasing elevation decreases temperature dramatically - every 1000' gain will cool the surroundings 3.5F. So when it's 100F on the Hassayampa River at 2000', it will be 80F on the Mogollon Rim at 8000'. And there is sunshine at least part of each day for more than 300 days a year. The diversity of vegetation and wildlife through the four climate-life zones from the desert to the Rim is stunning. So, with a little common sense, you can hike comfortably in any season and enjoy dramatic scenery and fascinating wildlife year 'round.

In the dead of the winter hiking's best at the lower elevations of 1000' to 4000', as found in the desert. You'll find bubbling winter streams east of Apache Junction in the Superstition Mountains (LaBarge Creek and Fish Creek), the hills north of Carefree (Cave Creek), and on the plains of Wickenburg at the Hassayampa River or at Burro Creek.

Spring offers pleasant hiking at intermediate elevations from 3000' to 6000'. It's an exciting time for streamside hikes, since melting winter snows charge dry stream beds and bring trickling waterfalls to full life. You'll find spectacular falls north of Globe in the Sierra Anchas (Workman Creek and Reynolds Creek) and around Payson (Barnhart Canyon and Ellison Creek). A list of waterfalls is given in Chapter 3. Some creeks are at their best in the spring, including ones by Sedona (Woods Canyon) and near Payson in the Mazatzals (Barnhart Canyon and Deer Creek) or by the Rim (Pine Creek and Ellison Creek).

In the heat of summer, it is most comfortable to hike streamside at higher elevations between 5000' and 8000'. Some easy and scenic lake shore hikes near Payson on top of the Mogollon Rim are Willow Springs Lake and Woods Canyon Lake. South of Prescott you'll find an alpine setting by Goldwater Lake and Lynx Lake. If you can take the heat, there are cool swimming holes at 3000' to 4000' along the Mogollon Rim transition region by Camp Verde (West Clear Creek, Wet Beaver Creek, and Sycamore Creek) and also by Payson (Fossil Springs and Water Wheel CG). A list of swimming holes is presented in Chapter 3.

Fall brings cool, crisp nights and clear, warm days at intermediate elevations from 3000' to 6000'. Hiking reveals spectacular scenery with an artist's palette of fall colors. Along perennial streams the backdrop of deep green pines and glossy green live oaks highlight the intense oranges and reds of box elders and mountain maples and accentuate the brilliant yellows of oaks, aspens, cottonwoods and sycamores. Some of the most colorful hikes are found just below the Rim by Sedona (West Fork and Woods Canyon), by Payson (See Canyon, Horton Creek, and Deer Creek), and near Camp Verde (Parsons Springs and Wet Beaver Creek).

Each season is not without its hazards. Winter rains and wind can easily cause hypothermia. Spring runoff and summer storms can cause flash floods, especially in narrow canyons. Summer heat, especially in a dry climate, can rapidly induce heat stroke. Fall can catch the unprepared hiker unaware with a late heat wave or early snow storm. Read more about this in Chapter 3 on Hiking Preparations and Precautions.

Chapter 3. Central Arizona Trails
Choosing A Hike

Conditioning

* Before taking up hiking, it is best to start conditioning by climbing stairs and walking a few miles a week. If you're over 35, or have special physical limitations, check with a physician before starting. If you haven't hiked before, start with easy trails and build up your strength, endurance, and confidence before moving on to more difficult trails.

What Type of Hike?

* Everyone's criteria for selecting hikes differs. Two of the most important factors are physical exertion and the wilderness experience. Physical factors such as endurance, exertion, and skill can be gauged by the hike's distance, steepness, elevation gain, and difficulty. Some want a workout, some prefer a stroll. For others, the wilderness experience is more important -- scenery, vistas, vegetation, and wildlife. We have suggested trails in the four major geographical regions which emphasize different aspects of the hiking experience: easier hikes, moderate hikes, more challenging hikes, and waterfall and swimming hole hikes. If you haven't hiked before, or if you haven't hiked in central Arizona, help prevent trouble by studying the sections on Hike Preparations and Hike Precautions.

Streamside Trails

* On any streamside trail you'll be hiking to, along, across, or in a body of water. You should decide what preparations are required if you inadvertently get wet, or maybe even if you want to deliberately get wet. On some trails, such as Aravaipa Creek, just plan on wading through the creek. So choose a time like fall or spring when it is warm, but not hot, and bring a change of footwear and a towel or, to be completely prepared, even a change of clothes. On many trails, such as West Fork of Oak Creek or Canyon Creek, you'll have to cross the creek many times. You might slip on a mossy rock into a few inches of water, so it won't hurt to have a change of shoes back at the car. Many other trails around lakes and along creeks only skirt the water, so you can just pace yourself, enjoy the scenery, and stay dry.

Factors in Choosing a Hike

* **Seasonal Weather** - Match the hike to your abilities and the season. In the winter look for open, exposed trails at the lower, warmer elevations less than 4500'. In the summer look for trails that are shaded and with higher, cooler elevations more than 4500'. Also try to avoid strenuous hiking in the intense, early afternoon sun.

* **Difficulty** - Everyone's criteria for rating hikes differs. Although the exertion (as characterized by distance and elevation gain) is a significant factor, the trail condition is also important. If the path is rocky or slippery, the hike may be more difficult than expected. Considering exertion alone, we have suggested guidelines for rating hikes for a moderately conditioned person -- one who plays tennis or walks five to ten miles a week and takes stairs:

> Easier - less than 6 miles and less than 1000' elevation gain
>
> Moderate - 6 to 12 miles and 1000' to 2000' elevation gain
>
> More Challenging - more than 12 miles and/or more than 2000' elevation gain.

* **Time** - Estimate the time for a hike from its distance and elevation change. A moderately well-conditioned hiker will require about 20 minutes for every mile and about 20 minutes for every 500' elevation gain. Times for individuals will vary significantly.

Maps

* **Regional maps** - The Forest Service issues maps for the National Forests where most of the hikes are located - Tonto NF, Coconino NF, and Prescott NF . They provide an overview of a large area (scale 1/2" = 1 mile) that covers 60 to 100 miles. They show Forest Service boundaries, wilderness boundaries, roads, and trails. Not all roads or trails are shown, but additional information may be obtained from the local Ranger District Station.

***Area maps** - There are excellent area maps for some locales which are listed below. The maps are available in most map and hiking stores. They cover a moderately sized area of 10 to 30 miles (scale 1" = 1 mile to 1.5" = 1 mile) and provide much information and detail on trailhead locations and hiking routes. A list of regional and area maps are given below.

East Central Arizona

I.   Apache Jct   - FS Tonto NF, FS Superstition Wilderness,
                   Earth Tracks Superstition West, John Schotts Phoenix Area

II. Globe   - FS Tonto NF, FS Sierra Ancha Wilderness,
                   Earth Tracks Sierra Anchas

Northeast Central Arizona

III. Payson South - FS Tonto NF, FS Mazatzal Wilderness, Schotts Mazatazal Mtns

IV.   Payson East - FS Tonto NF, Earth Tracks Mogollon Rim West,
                    Earth Tracks Mogollon Rim East, AZ Highways Mogollon Rim
                    John Schotts Mogollon Rim

V.   Payson West - FS Tonto NF, FS Mazatzal Wilderness,
                    Earth Tracks Mogollon Rim West, John Schotts Mogollon Rim

North Central Arizona

VI.   Carefree   - FS Tonto NF, John Schotts Phoenix Area

VII. Camp Verde   - FS Coconino NF, John Schotts Prescott NF

VIII. Sedona   - FS Coconino NF, Thorne Enterprises Experience Sedona
                    Earth Tracks Sedona

Northwest Central Arizona

IX. Prescott   - FS Prescott NF, John Schotts Prescott NF

X.   Wickenburg   - BLM Wickenburg

* **US Geological Survey Topographical Maps** - Popular trails have clearly marked and well-maintained paths. However, more isolated trails may require orienteering. USGS topographic 7.5° maps, which cover seven by nine miles (scale 3" = 1 mile), are useful for charting the trail direction, distance, elevation gain, steepness, and hazards. These maps are also useful for checking out the potential for vistas and views.

* **Map Sources** - The most convenient way to obtain maps is to purchase them from a retail map shop or hiking store. Potential sources in Phoenix include Wide World of Maps, REI Outfitters, and The Hiking Shack. Maps of the National Forests and Wilderness Areas may be purchased directly from the National Forest Service, eg. in Phoenix at Tonto National Forest Headquarters on McDowell Rd. The USGS maps can be ordered directly from the United States Geological Survey. The National Forest and USGS maps cost from $2 to $4 each while the specialized area maps that are produced commercially cost from $2 to $6 each.

Easier Hikes

In a land of dryness, water is often worth its weight in gold. So it was that early prospectors sometimes took the rewards of their claim and then left when water dried up, even if some rich diggings remained. Today, both the novice and veteran hiker will appreciate the new rewards that streamside trails offer in stimulating the senses. The sights, sounds, and smells triggered by flowing waters will keep a trekker waiting for each new surprise around every mysterious bend in the trail. Compared to a dry wash, a riparian stream has many times the variety of vegetation and bird species, which further expands the diversity of sensations. You'll enjoy streamside hiking in Central Arizona's four regions which have environments that vary from cool, fir-forested mountains down to the warm, cactus-dotted desert plain.

In the Eastern Region the spring thaw in the rugged Sierra Anchas uncovers pale-green grassy meadows and coaxes forth golden-green aspen leaves. North of Globe you'll find mossy-rocked streams like Workman Creek and Reynolds Creek. In the Northeastern Region the Mogollon Rim's melting snows charge mineral laden springs that feed the region's numerous creeks. West of Payson you can savor cool mists drifting from cascading waterfalls on trails like Ellison Creek or the East Verde Water Wheel. The Northern Region is drier and has fewer perennial creeks running from the Rim. Still, the tenderfoot can hike short distances near Sedona and enjoy wading into broad shallows or splashing into deep pools along Oak Creek trails such as Slide Rock or West Fork. In the Northwestern Region the moisture in the craggy Bradshaw Mountains runs to local lakes, or beyond, on a long route out to the desert plain. Near Prescott, city folk can enjoy alpine vistas while hiking or fishing by the tall, narrow pines at locations such as Lynx Lake and Goldwater Lake.

The easier hikes in Central Arizona are listed on the adjoining page. The trail access and exertion level are reasonable, so they are a good start for inexperienced, younger, and older hikers. They are also well traveled, not strenuous, and don't require great dexterity. Although these trails may be easier than others, they are not trivial, because you are still venturing into nature. You must prepare properly, BRING WATER, and do not hike alone.

Cool, leisurely stroll awaits trekkers on route around Woods Canyon Lake.

18

Easier Hikes

Area II. Globe Vicinity Trails

4 - Workman Crk -Tubs   - Very short, steep path to small tiered waterfall.
5 - Workman Crk-Forest   - Short, cool forest stroll by creek lined with mossy rocks.

Area IV. Payson East Vicinity Trails

14 - Christopher Cr-Box Cn   - Nice walk down to cascades in deep, chiseled basalt canyon.
20 - Willow Springs Lake   - Watch fishermen test luck on pine forest lake shore walk.
21 - Woods Canyon Lake   - Stroll as far as you want on five mile route around Rim lake.
22 -East Chevelon Creek   - Small creek winds thru grassy meadow in shallow canyon
23 - Bear Canyon Lake   - Steep descent to easy trail that leads to peninsula in lake.

Area V. Payson West Vicinity Trails

24 - E. Verde - Water Wheel   - Short walk on sandy bank to tall, tiered waterfall and pool.
25 - Ellison Creek   - Mile walk on jeep trail to sloped cascading waterfall.
26 - E. Verde - Flowing Spr   - Easy stroll along banks & meadows of red rock canyon.

Area VII. Camp Verde Vicinity Trails

37 - Rarick Canyon   - Short, isolated trail runs to spring time pools and beyond.
38 - Wet Beaver Crk - Bell Trl - Warm walk near creek to wading and swimming area.

Area VIII. Sedona Vicinity Trails

39 -Oak Creek - Allen's Bend - Short, cool forest stroll along creek with pools and cascades.
40 - Oak Creek - Slide Rock   - Slippery chutes for sliding down red rock slabs.
41 - West Fork Oak Creek   - Walk across shallow creek in area's most scenic canyon.
43 - Oak Creek - Red Rock   - Classic view of Old West symbol - Cathedral Rock.
44 - Oak Creek - Kisva Trl   - Nice streamside stroll in Red Rock State Park.

Area IX. Prescott Vicinity Trails

45 - Watson Lake   - Scenic views, but hard walking at lake by Granite Dells.
46 - Goldwater Lake   - Walk up to three miles around lake by Prescott City Park.
47 - Lynx Lake   - Easy undulating trail around cobalt waters of alpine lake.

Area X. Wickenburg Vicinity Trails

49 - Hassayampa Preserve   - Stroll around showplace desert riparian environment.

Moderate Hikes

The pleasure of a streamside hike may be in the sights and sounds of the journey: water splashing over a random, rocky cascade; fuzzy green moss creeping up a rock-lined creek bank; or a blue heron resting in a shallow, rippling pool. The delight might also be in that special destination - a refracting waterfall tumbling over a precipice, a quiet pool crowded by yellow columbine, or a swimming hole framed by tiered, red-rock slabs. Moderate hikes involve trekkers with their surroundings or reward them with special pleasures at trail's end. Each of the four major geographical regions has its own characteristic beauty, so there's always a good answer to the question "Does it ever get any better than this?"

In East Central Arizona the low, hot, craggy Superstitions come to life with winter rains. Beyond Apache Junction the intermediate hiker can wade the cool shallows of Fish Creek into a deep luxurious canyon. In Northeast Central Arizona a variety of discoveries await the curious hiker around Payson. To the south yellow columbine bathe in patches of dappled light streaming through creekside sycamores on the Little Saddle Mountain Trail. To the east one can see white-breasted nut hatches buzzing through the pines en route to a gushing waterfall on the Gordon Creek Trail. In North Central Arizona, where rainfall becomes more scarce along the Rim, water from a few larger, longer creeks has carved winding canyons and deep pools during the descent from the Rim to the desert plain. Near Camp Verde you'll enjoy red rock-scenery en route to swimming holes on the sparkling waters of Wet Beaver Creek and West Clear Creek Trails.

Some of the moderate hikes in Central Arizona are listed on the adjoining page. These routes are referred to as moderate for a variety of reasons. They may require greater exertion, but may also require dexterity because of obstacles, such as ledges, boulders, or slippery rocks. Some pathfinding may be required if trail access is not marked or if a trail itself is undesignated, unmaintained, or primitive. So these trails should be hiked by those with some experience or with an experienced friend. Even if you are a veteran trekker, these hikes are not trivial, so you must still prepare properly, BRING WATER, and do not hike alone.

Hikers head up through grassy meadow on Little Saddle Mountain Trail.

20

Moderate Hikes

Area I. Apache Junction Vicinity Trails

1 - LaBarge Crk-Boulder Can - Moderate climb to boulder-filled winter creek.
3 - Fish Creek-Lower - Walk in water on primitive trail into deep, scenic canyon.

Area II. Globe Vicinity Trails

8 - Aravaipa Creek - Breathtaking water walk into lush, deep, unique canyon.

Area III. Payson South Vicinity Trails

9 - Little Saddle Mountain - Semishaded spring hike by small stream to minifalls.
10 - Deer Creek - Hilly, but refreshing hike along spring time creek.
12 - Tonto Crk-Indian Farm - Cross country walk to Narrows on Tonto Creek.

Area IV. Payson East Vicinity Trails

15 - Hunter Creek - Open meadow walk by shallow stream with crawdad pools.
16 - Gordon Creek - Pine forests, grassy meadows, and rocky bank lead to falls.
17 - Horton Creek - Moderate hike to mountainside spring gushing into pool.
18 -Christopher Crk-See Can - Maples and oaks refreshing in spring and colorful in fall.
19 - Canyon Creek - Rock hop across creek in flowery high mountain meadow.

Area V. Payson West Vicinity Trails

27 - East Webber Creek - Fine variety of birds, butterflies & trees on uphill walk.
30 - Fossil Creek Bridge - Short scramble to aqua waters of travertine swim hole.
31 - Verde River - Hot Springs - Wade across Verde to hot spring in ruins of old resort.

Area VI. Carefree Vicinity Trails

32 -Verde River-Needle Rock - Hilly route along Verde on old jeep trail to Horseshoe Dam.
33 -Cave Creek Trail - Long hilly trail with a few nice swimming holes.
34 -Verde Riv-Sheep Bridge - Bridge offers fine vistas of Mazatzals and Verde River.

Area VII. Camp Verde Vicinity Trails

35 - Sycamore Cr-Parson Spr - Easy descent leads to a couple of deep swim holes.
36 - West Clear Creek - Warm hike to nice spots for a dip in red rock canyon.

Area VIII. Sedona Vicinity Trails

42 - Dry Beaver Cr-Wood Can - Dry creek regains vigor in spring from snow melt.

Area IX. Prescott Vicinity Trails

48 - Hassayampa Lake - Aspen and fir whistle with gentlest breeze at lake's edge.

Area X. Wickenburg Vicinity Trails

50 - Burro Creek - Flat, rocky walk may be rewarded with wildlife sightings.

More Challenging Hikes

Your ankles are aching, your legs are throbbing, and your foot has just twisted off another slippery creek bed rock. You glance ahead and a branch pokes at your eyes. You begin to wonder what was so special about that isolated, sheltered swim hole still more than a mile away. More challenging streamside trails present special types of difficulties to the hardier hiker. Traditionally, difficult trails require endurance for distance and strength for steep grades. But streamside trails also require dexterity for overcoming obstacles and courage for confronting unknown hazards. Proper preparation, conditioning, and pacing are required to minimize risk and maximize pleasure. Each of the four geographical regions has watery landscapes that present their own unique challenges.

In the Eastern Region, the volcanic outcroppings of the Superstition Mountains are drained of winter rains by creeks running through rocky, brushy canyons. East of Apache Junction, Fish Creek sits at the bottom of a thousand foot deep canyon and challenges the experienced hiker to miniadventures in bouldering, ledge walking, and creek crossing. In the Sierra Anchas northeast of Globe, veterans will enjoy two of the most difficult streamside trails. Along Reynolds Creek, both the Falls Trail and Hells Hole Trail have distances that are long, inclines that are steep, and scenery that is spectacular. In the Northeastern Region near Payson, steep grades guard scenic spots on the Barnhart, Fossil Springs, and Pine Creek Trails. In the Northern Region, endurance is required for long creeks and dexterity is demanded for creek crossing and walking. You can test these skills near Carefree on the Cave Creek Trail and near Camp Verde on the Wet Clear Creek and Wet Beaver Creek Trails.

Some of the more challenging hikes in Central Arizona are listed on the adjoining page. Some trails are difficult because of their length and steepness, but others require special skills; pathfinding, boulder clambering, ledge walking, and creek hiking. These trails are often isolated and are best attempted by well seasoned veterans hiking together. The physical intensity and endurance of such a hike are rewarded with solitude, scenery, and satisfaction. Make sure to leave word of your plans and your return schedule. As always, prepare properly, BRING WATER, and do not hike alone.

Ten miles of rolling hills challenges hikers on the Cave Creek Trail

22

More Challenging Hikes

Area I. Apache Junction Vicinity Trails
2 - Fish Cr-Upper Can - Creek crossing, boulder clambering, ledge walking effort.

3 - Fish Cr-Lower Can - Longer in-stream hike reveals spectacular canyon scenery.

Area II. Globe Vicinity Trails
6 - Reynolds-Hellshole - Strenuous up and down hike to scenic canyon narrows.

7 - Reynolds Cr-Falls - Very steep hike to falls and pine, fir, & aspen forests beyond.

8 - Aravaipa Canyon - Hike in and out of scenic canyon 10 or 15 miles in a day.

Area III. Payson South Vicinity Trails
10 -Deer Creek Trail - Tough, but scenic ten miler up to summit of Mt. Peeley.

11 - Barnhart Trail - Strenuous effort up to hidden spring time falls at 3 miles.

Area IV. Payson East Vicinity Trails
13 - Tonto Cr-Bear Flat - Tough creek walking, boulder clambering, and bushwhacking.

Area V. Payson West Vicinity Trails
28 - Pine Creek Trail - Steep switchbacks down to cool, lush creek under the Rim.

29 - Fossil Springs Trl - Dusty grade down to refreshing million gallon/hour springs.

Area VI. Carefree Vicinity Trails
33 -Cave Creek Trail - Scenic, hilly 10 mile effort requires good conditioning.

Area VII. Camp Verde Vicinity Trails
36 - West Clear Creek - Creek crossings and deep pools will challenge beyond 3 miles.

38 - Beaver Cr-Bell Trl - Wade on slippery rocks past 2-miles for new red rock scenes.

Area VIII. Sedona Vicinity Trails
41 - West Fork-Oak Cr - Wade & swim to new red rock delights beyond the 3-mile point.

Waterfall & Swimming Hole Hikes

What is so fascinating about flowing waters? You can hear the freshness of a spring creek's melted winter snows splashing over a cascade or the power of a flooded river roaring through its rapids. You can gaze at a waterfall misting a glistening canyon wall or waves washing deepening hues into dusty red-rock slabs. You can sniff the pungent smell of a shallow, isolated pool or the sweet air of a percolating spring. And you can taste the bitter flavor of a sulfurous hot spring or the metallic tang of a forest spring. Not least of all is the refreshment of wading into a shallow, cool stream or the shock of plunging into a deep, icy pool. The sensations of streamside hiking are intensified with the sight of a waterfall or feeling of a swim. You'll find such experiences in the four regions of central Arizona.

In the Eastern Region the rugged Sierra Anchas' slopes may steepen into vertically planed cliffs that can transform mundane creeks into spectacular falls. North of Globe, the Workman Creek and Reynolds Creek falls are spectacular in the spring, but still pleasant in the summer. In the Northeastern Region, near Payson, the dropoff along the Mogollon Rim gives rise to waterfalls among the pines with falls along Ellison, Christopher, Gordon, and Canyon Creeks. You can also cool off at deep pools along these creeks and at Fossil Creek, East Verde River, and Verde Hot Springs. In the Northern Region spring waters have cut long, deep, serpentine paths through ancient sedimentary layers. Near Sedona and Camp Verde, red rock slabs line the banks of spacious, quiet swimming holes along Oak Creek, West Clear Creek, Wet Beaver Creek, and Sycamore Creek.

The most inviting waterfall and swimming hole hikes in Central Arizona are listed on the adjoining page. Most waterfalls are best during spring snow melt or summer monsoons. Swim holes are well charged in late spring, but some shrink during summer. Although refreshing, many miles of hot hiking may be required, so don't forget water and sunscreen. It's also best to use footwear while swimming to avoid the chance of cuts from debris. In spite of these worries, nothing refreshes more than a cool dip in clear water on a hot summer day. As usual, you must still prepare properly, BRING WATER, and do not hike alone.

Rock hopping rewards trekkers with sight of waterfall on Ellison Creek.

Waterfall Hikes

Area II. Globe Vicinity Trails

4 - Workman Crk-The Tubs - Easy scramble down to small tiered waterfall in glen.
5 - Workman Crk-Forest Trl - Small creek slides from forest down 200' precipice.
7 - Reynolds Creek-The Falls - Steep hike to thin ribbon of a waterfall, best in spring.

Area III. Payson South Vicinity Trails

11 - Barnhart Canyon - Uphill 3 mile climb to hidden 50' spring time waterfall.

Area IV. Payson East Vicinity Trails

16 - Gordon Creek - Flat, then rocky, 3-mile hike to 30' falls plunging into pool.

Area V. Payson West Vicinity Trails

2 4 - East Verde-Water Wheel - Short, easy walk on sandy bank to tall, two-tiered waterfall.
2 5 - Ellison Creek - Moderate, 1-mile walk down to 40' cascading waterfall.

Swimming Hole Hikes

Area II. Globe Vicinity Trails

8 - Aravaipa Canyon - The creek has carved nice, deep pools in this scenic canyon.

Area IV. Payson East Vicinity Trails

14 - Christopher Crk-Box Can - Easy walk to creek, tricky walking in slippery, tiered pools.
1 6 - Gordon Creek - Flat, then rocky, 3-mile hike to 30' falls plunging into pool.

Area V. Payson West Vicinity Trails

2 4 - East Verde-Water Wheel - Easy, 1/4 mile walk on sandy bank to clear water swim hole
2 9 - Fossil Springs - Steep, tough 3-mile walk to million gallon/hour 72F spring.
3 0 - Fossil Creek-Bridge Trail - Short scramble down to mini-Havasupai travertine pool.
3 1 - Verde River - Hot Springs - Easy, 1-mile walk & wade across Verde to hot spring ruins.

Area VI. Carefree Vicinity Trails

3 3 -Cave Creek Trail - Warm, hilly hike to a couple of nice swimming holes.

Area VII. Camp Verde Vicinity Trails

3 5 - Sycamore Crk-Parson Spr - Moderate semishaded walk to swim spots at 2 and 4 miles.
3 6 - West Clear Creek - Hot, easy walk to pools at 3 and 4 miles.
3 8 - Wet Beaver Crk-Bell Trail - Easy 2-mile trek to red rock shallows and pools.

Area VIII. Sedona Vicinity Trails

3 9 - Oak Creek-Allens Bend - Short, cool forest stroll on creek with pools and cascades.
4 0 - Oak Creek-Slide Rock - Slide down slick, red rock chutes in Oak Creek Canyon.
4 3 - Oak Creek-Red Rock Trail - Enjoy wading and splashing by historic Cathedral Rock.

Day Hiking Preparations

Clothing

* **Feet** - Help prevent blisters by wearing a very light second pair of socks. Wear sturdy, comfortable shoes that are broken in. Lightweight hiking shoes are best because they are ventilated and they also provide protection against cacti, rocks, and ankle twists. Jogging shoes may be adequate for easier trails, but tennis shoes are not recommended for any trail because they slide on gravel and slip on damp rocks.

* **Head** - Wear a hat to shield your eyes from the sun. It also cools your head when it's warm and warms it when its cool. Suntan lotion reduces burns and sunglasses reduce glare.

* **Upper bod** - Wear layers and strip them as the day warms up. A lightweight poncho in the pack is good for sudden squalls and helps prevent hypothermia on cool, windy, rainy days. Thin, long sleeve shirts are good for protecting against sunburn, insect bites, cuts, scratches, and poison ivy. They are also good for staying warm on cool days.

* **Lower bod** - Long pants are generally best since they protect against cuts, scratches, poison ivy, and insect bites. If you take a familiar or well used trail with little overgrowth, shorts may be fine on warmer days, but don't forget to lather up with suntan lotion.

Sustenance

* **BRING ENOUGH WATER.** - In the desert you can survive a week without food, but exerting yourself in hot weather without water can cause heatstroke in less than half a day. On hot days bring at least one quart for every 5 miles and every 1000' elevation gain. To help prevent cramps mix half water and half electrolyte (eg.Gatorade). For hikes extending beyond a day, more water or alternate sources are required. Don't drink from open sources!

* **Food** - A few sandwiches and a piece of fruit are good for a day hiking lunch. On longer hikes trail mix, or trail mix bars, make a nice snack supplement during breaks.

Day Packs

* **General** - Good day packs and miscellaneous gear make hiking easier and more enjoyable. Borrow or buy a cheap day pack if you're not sure you want to become a hiker. If you hike often, better gear will serve you better. Here are some items you can purchase.

* **Fanny pack** - A small pack that straps on the waist and is useful for short to moderate day hikes. It's easier to use than a shoulder harness day pack because it takes stress off the shoulders. Make sure it has room for water, lunch, and a few emergency supplies.

* **Shoulder day pack** - Lightweight shoulder packs are best if they have well padded straps and a waist belt to help take weight off the shoulders and shift it to the hips. Water is more accessible if the pack has external water bottle pouches or a place to hook up pouches.

* **Water pouches** - These fit onto your belt or pack and provide easy access to H2O.

* **Camera pouches** - These fit onto your belt to minimize the hassle of taking pictures.

Utility Kit

* **Pack** - Small utility packs with many pockets and elastic holders are available in most hiking stores. They are very useful for gathering together in one place first aid, medication, emergency supplies, and miscellaneous goods. Some useful items include the following.

* **First aid** - Items frequently found in backpacks include moleskin for blisters, band-aids for cuts and scratches, stretch tape for sprains, cortisone lotion (eg. Cortaid) for itchy insect bites and scratches. Sun screen (SPF 15 or more) and lip balm for hot weather.

* **Medication** - Antihistamines, antacids, aspirins, and any other personal medication.

* **Odds & ends** - Long toothed comb for removing cactus balls, a small needle-nosed pliers for removing cactus needles, and a tweezers for removing very fine cactus needles. A Swiss army knife for utility use. Other items include; flashlight, compass, mirror, whistle, insect repellent, waterproof matches and case, and toilet paper. And don't forget your map!

Day Hiking Precautions

Before You Depart

* Plan to hike with a partner, especially on isolated trails and in the back country.
* Let someone know of your starting point, destination, and estimated time of return.
* Leave your valuables at home.
* Take a spare key for your car.

Weather

* **General** - Weather is more likely to kill a hiker than is falling off a cliff. Take precautions against heatstroke in hot weather, hypothermia in cool and wet weather, and lightning and flash floods in stormy weather. Check the weather reports. It can be 80° in January or 40° in May. Thunderstorms are likely from mid-June to mid-September and rain and snow are quite possible from December to February.

* **Hot weather** - To stay cooler and help to avoid overexposure and heatstroke, go to higher altitudes (above 4500') and shaded trails. BRING PLENTY OF WATER and use a hat, suntan lotion, and sunglasses.

* **Cool weather** - To stay warmer, go to lower altitudes (below 4500') and more open trails. Cooler weather becomes dangerous when it is also wet and windy -- hypothermia becomes possible. Cancel a hike if the weather looks really bad. Otherwise, bring a waterproof poncho, hat and gloves, and wear layers for warmth and flexibility.

* **Stormy weather** - Lightning and flash floods are real hazards on streamside hikes. Trees can sizzle from a lightning strike. During the monsoon season from mid-June to mid-September, hike early in the day to avoid storms which roll in by mid-afternoon. To help avoid lightning, avoid open places and tall trees. To help avoid flash floods, don't park in sandy washes and don't hike in narrow canyons.

Nasty Botany

* **Cacti** - Avoid them. Just as a precaution, bring a long toothed comb to pull out cactus balls, a needle-nosed pliers for big needles, and a tweezers for small needles.

* **Thorny brush** - A hat, long sleeved shirt, and long pants will minimize scratches.

* **Poison ivy** - These plants take the shape of vines, shrubs, and ground cover. They are often found in moist cooler locations along stream banks and in the upper portions of canyons. Avoid them. Three leaves from a stem are one sign of poison ivy and oak. Other signs are glossy leaves and bright colors in late summer and fall. Cortisone cream (eg. Cortaid) helps with minor contact. Contact a physician for severe cases.

Critters

*Rattlesnakes - They want to be left alone so just avoid them. They enjoy moderate temperatures, so you're more likely to encounter them when hiking is also more comfortable. Keep your eyes on the trail and on nearby brush. Scuffing the ground to make noise helps to not surprise them. People rarely die if bitten by a rattler, although children and dogs are at greater risk. If you are bitten, stay quiet and send for help. There are different approaches to treating bites. If you are worried, check with your physician or the National Forest Service before you depart on your hike.

* **Scorpions** - Don't pick up a rock or a branch without turning it over first. Although it's unlikely, you might find a scorpion underneath. Scorpion fatalities are rare, but the sting is at least painful and numbing. If stung, stay calm. If there is a significant reaction, send someone for help. Antivenins, if necessary, are available at clinics and hospitals.

* **Spiders** - Don't reach behind rocks or between crevices. As with other poisonous critters, the stings are rarely fatal, but can swell and cause pain and nausea for a day or two. If stung, stay calm. If there is a significant reaction, send someone for help. Again, antivenins, if necessary, are available at clinics and hospitals.

27

Environmental Courtesy

Appreciate the Environment

* Leave flowers, rocks, wood, wildlife signs, and other pleasures for other hikers to enjoy. Removing anything is against the law, although local consumption of dead wood for campfires is allowed (when fire danger is low). Please leave a picnic site or a campsite in at least as good, if not better, condition than you found it.

Appreciate the Antiquities

* Don't deface rocks, petroglyphs, or pictographs with graffiti; these records of ancient civilizations survived the last 800 to 3000 years and shouldn't be altered or lost.

Appreciate Wilderness Areas

* The Federal Government has protected a million acres of land in Arizona and you can do your share to help preserve the environment. When hiking, limit group size to no more than 15 people. Leave mountain bikes, ATV's, and 4-wheel vehicles at the trailhead. All mechanized vehicles are prohibited in wilderness areas.

Appreciate the Trails

* Don't litter - pack out everything you brought in. Don't even throw away apple cores or orange peels. They are not eaten by wildlife and may take hundreds of years to degrade. Think about taking out a stray tin can or piece of trash that isn't yours. If you must smoke, pack out your cigarette butts. If there is a fire hazard, don't even consider smoking. Avoid cutting across switchbacks; it disrupts fragile vegetation and speeds erosion.

Appreciate Other Hikers

* Avoid degrading the wilderness experience with screaming, shooting guns or playing amplified music.

Respect Private Property

* Avoid trouble by not trespassing or littering private land and not parking in driveways.

Appreciate the National Forest Service

* The National Forest Service monitors, maintains, and preserves the wilderness resources. They care about the environment, but have to spend a significant amount of time housecleaning areas that are poorly cared for by visitors. Do what you can to assist them in their efforts to preserve the resources of an area by packing refuse out, even picking some up that isn't yours. They are willing to provide friendly assistance with directions or information about locations or availability of activities in the area. So support your local ranger. You can call, visit, or write the National Forest at the locations listed on the adjoining page.

Federal, State, & Local Agencies

Bureau of Land Management

Phoenix District Office, 2015 W. Deer Valley Rd, Phoenix AZ 85027 - (602) 726-6300

Safford District Office, 425 E. 4th Street, Safford AZ - (520) 428-4040

United States Forest Service

Apache-Sitgreaves National Forest (520) 333-4301
P.O. Box 640, Springerville AZ 86435

Chevelon Ranger District, 1520 W. 3rd Street, Winslow AZ 86047 (520) 289-2471

Coconino National Forest (520) 527-7400
2323 Greenlaw Lane, Flagstaff, AZ 86001,

Beaver Creek Ranger District, H.C. 64, Box 240, Rimrock AZ 86335 - (520) 567-4501

Sedona Ranger Station, Ranger Road, P.O. Box 300, Sedona AZ 86336 - (520) 282-4119

Prescott National Forest (520) 445-1762
334 South Cortez Street, P.O.Box 2549, Prescott AZ 86301

Bradshaw Ranger District, 2230 E. Hwy 69, Prescott AZ 86301- (520) 445-7253

Tonto National Forest (602) 261-3205
102 S. 28th Street, P.O.Box 29070, Phoenix AZ 85038

Cave Creek Ranger District, P.O. Box 5068, Carefree AZ 85377 - (602) 488-3441

Globe Ranger District, Route 1 Box 33, Globe AZ 85501 - (520) 425-7189

Mesa Ranger Dist., P.O. Box 5800, 26 N. McDonald, Mesa AZ 85211 - (602) 835-1161

Payson Ranger District, 1009 E. Hwy 260, Payson AZ 85541 - (520) 474-2269

Pleasant Valley Ranger District, P.O. Box 450, Young AZ 85554 - (520) 462-3311

Tonto Basin R. D., St Hwy 88, PO Box 649, Roosevelt AZ 85545 - (520) 467-2236

State Agencies

Slide Rock State Park, P.O. Box 10358, Sedona AZ 86339 - (520) 282-3034

Red Rock State Park, H.C.-02, P.O. Box 886, Sedona AZ 86336 - (520) 282-6907

Local Agencies

City of Prescott Recreation Services, P.O. Box 2059, Prescott AZ 86302- (520) 776-6285

The Nature Conservancy - Hassayampa River Preserve
PO Box 1162, Wickenburg AZ 85358 - (520) 684-2772

East Central Arizona Trails

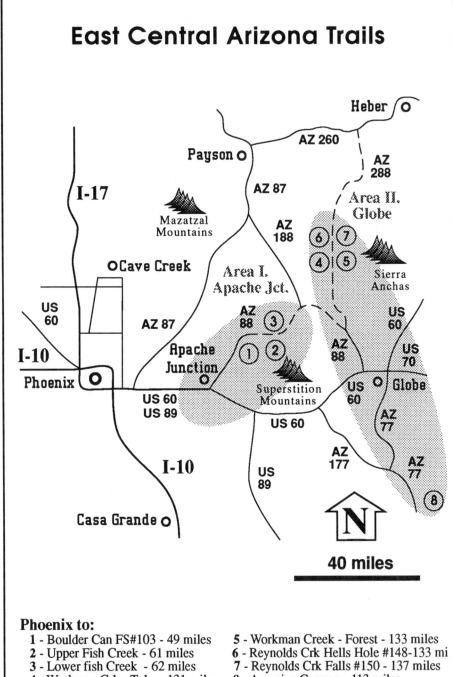

Phoenix to:

1 - Boulder Can FS#103 - 49 miles
2 - Upper Fish Creek - 61 miles
3 - Lower fish Creek - 62 miles
4 - Workman Crk - Tubs - 131 miles
5 - Workman Creek - Forest - 133 miles
6 - Reynolds Crk Hells Hole #148 -133 mi
7 - Reynolds Crk Falls #150 - 137 miles
8 - Aravaipa Canyon - 113 miles

Ch. 4. East Central Arizona Trails

Area I. Apache Junction Vicinity

1 - LaBarge Creek - Boulder Canyon Trail FS#103
2 - Fish Creek - Upper Canyon Trail
3 - Fish Creek - Lower Canyon Trail

Area II. Globe Vicinity

4 - Workman Creek - The Tubs Trail
5 - Workman Creek - The Forest Trail
6 - Reynolds Creek - Hells Hole Trail FS#148
7 - Reynolds Creek - The Falls Trail FS#150
8 - Aravaipa Canyon Trail

Southern Superstitions are framed by arch along Fish Creek Canyon

Area I. Apache Junction Trails

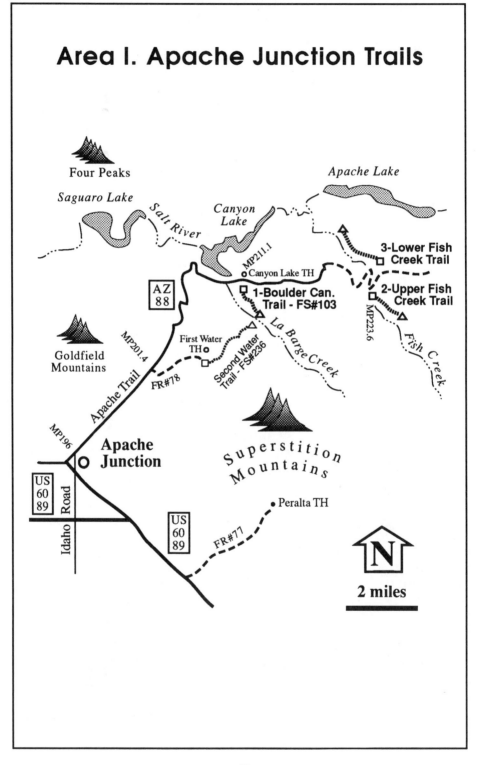

Four Peaks

Apache Lake

Saguaro Lake

Salt River

Canyon Lake

3-Lower Fish Creek Trail

MP211.1

Canyon Lake TH

2-Upper Fish Creek Trail

AZ 88

1-Boulder Can. Trail - FS#103

MP223.6

La Barge Creek

Fish Creek

MP201.4

First Water TH

Goldfield Mountains

Second Water Trail - FS#236

Apache Trail

FR#78

MP196

Apache Junction

Superstition Mountains

US 60 89

Idaho Road

• Peralta TH

US 60 89

FR#77

N

2 miles

Area I.
Apache Junction Vicinity

HIKE DESCRIPTIONS & LOCAL MAPS

1 - LaBarge Creek - Boulder Canyon Trail FS#103
2 - Fish Creek - Upper Canyon Trail
3 - Fish Creek - Lower Canyon Trail

Hikers water walk into scenic Lower Fish Creek Canyon.

Apache Junction Vicinity

1 - Boulder Canyon Trail FS#103

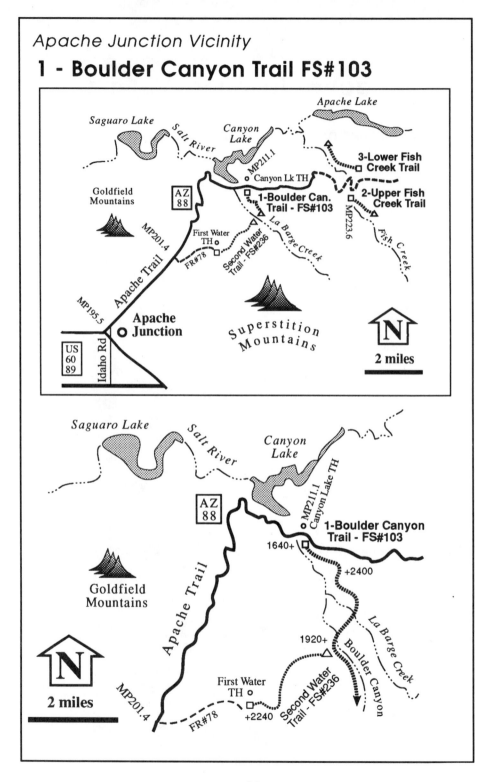

<u>1</u> - La Barge Creek - Boulder Canyon Trail FS#103

* Hilly hike to winter creek leads to fine scenery & rock hopping fun.

Canyon Lake TH to LaBarge Creek
3.0 mi; 800' gain

Special: Superstition Wilderness

Location:	Apache Jct - 16 miles NE
Elevation:	1640'
Seasons:	Dec - Mar
Agency:	Tonto NF - Mesa RD
Topo map:	Mormon Flat Dam

Gold fever has long affected prospectors in the Superstition Mountains, including a Frenchman named LaBarge, for whom the creek was named. He camped at a spring by Weavers Needle in the 1880s and knew Jacob Waltz, the Dutchman. Waltz regularly went into town to buy goods with gold, but died in 1898 without revealing the source. LaBarge spent most of the of his life and resources searching for Waltz's fabled Lost Dutchman Mine. His disappointment has been echoed by many others since then, even to the present.

The three mile hike on Boulder Canyon Trail to LaBarge Creek is a moderate, but exposed trek. The trail offers an early challenge with an 800' high hill, but then rewards the hiker with panoramic views of Canyon Lake and the eastern Superstitions. At 2.5 miles you'll pass the ruins of Indian Paint Mine, just another abandoned mine shaft that some gold digger sweated over long ago. At three miles you'll arrive at LaBarge Creek - hot and dusty in the summer, but cool, wet, and refreshing in the winter. You can relax, listen to the splashing water, and enjoy the scenery, including the massive, tawny Battleship Mountain rising to the south. Or, you can go rock hopping along the bank for as long as your ankles hold out. The creek can also be accessed by a three-mile hike on Second Water Trail which originates at First Water Trailhead.

<u>**Directions to Trailhead**</u>: **From Apache Junction, at Apache Trail (AZ 88) and Idaho Road, go NE 16 miles on AZ 88 to Canyon Lake Marina (MP211.1). Park in the marina lot and cross the road to the Canyon Lake TH.**

Winter rains splash along the rock filled bed of LaBarge Creek.

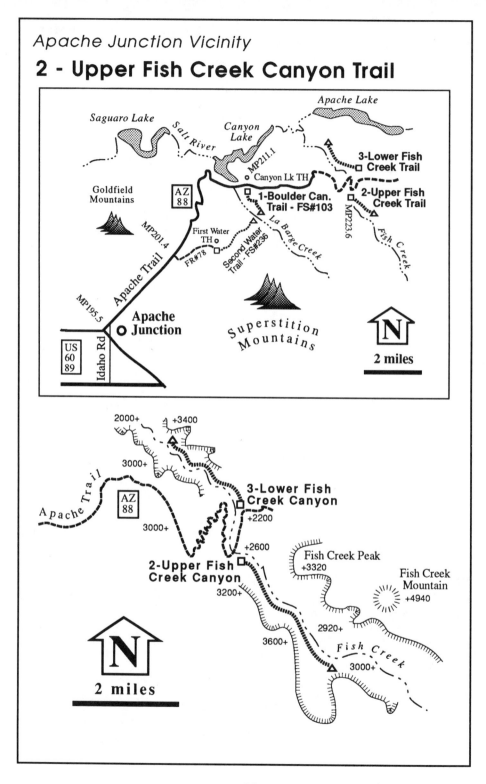

Apache Lake

Saguaro Lake

Canyon Lake

Salt River

MP211.1

Canyon Lk TH

3-Lower Fish Creek Trail

Goldfield Mountains

AZ 88

1-Boulder Can. Trail - FS#103

2-Upper Fish Creek Trail

MP201.4

First Water TH

La Barge Creek

MP223.6

Fish Creek

Apache Trail

FR#78

Second Water Trail - FS#236

MP195.5

Apache Junction

Superstition Mountains

N

2 miles

US 60 89

Idaho Rd

2000+   +3400

3000+

Apache Trail

AZ 88

3-Lower Fish Creek Canyon

+2200

3000+

+2600

2-Upper Fish Creek Canyon

Fish Creek Peak
+3320

Fish Creek Mountain
+4940

3200+

2920+

3600+

Fish Creek

3000+

N

2 miles

<u>2</u> - Fish Creek - Upper Canyon Trail

* Tough bouldering on primitive trail by winter creek in deep canyon..

AZ88 TH to creek pools **3.0 mi; 200' gain**	**Location:** Apache Jct - 28 miles NE **Elevation:** 2600' **Seasons:** Dec - Mar **Agency:** Tonto NF - Mesa RD
Special: Superstition Wilderness	**Topo map:** Horse Mesa Dam

The western frontier expanded only as fast as the government could supply soldiers and build forts to protect settlers from Indian attacks. When the Civil War began, most Union troops were withdrawn and many forts were burned. The Indians, believing they had won the war, increased the intensity and frequency of their attacks against the interlopers. So settlers would band together for punitive expeditions against the hostiles. One such foray, led by local rancher King Woolsey in 1864, encountered a band of Apaches in Fish Creek Canyon. A treacherous battle occurred when leaders from both sides, still carrying concealed weapons, met under a flag of truce. Woolsey signaled for an ambush first and some 40 Indians were killed in the ensuing fight that has become known as the Battle of Bloody Tanks.

Hiking along upper Fish Creek Canyon will reveal the rugged terrain that the Indians and the settlers once traversed. The primitive trail is a sometimes easy, sometimes challenging obstacle course. To reach a reflecting pool at two miles you'll teeter on slippery rocks across the creek, clamber and slide over barn-sized boulders, and abrade your body moving along three-foot wide ledges. The hike is not strenuous, but is not for novices. The reward is the spectacular beauty of a thousand foot deep canyon. It is a very peaceful place today.

Directions to Trail Access: From Apache Junction, at Apache Trail (AZ88) and Idaho Road, go NE 28 miles on AZ 88 to the bottom of Fish Creek Hill (MP223.6). Park at road side. Take a primitive trail just before the bridge on the south side and head up a hill to a cave, then down again to the creek bed.

Hikers scramble down slope into scenic Upper Fish Creek Canyon.

3 - Lower Fish Creek Canyon Trail

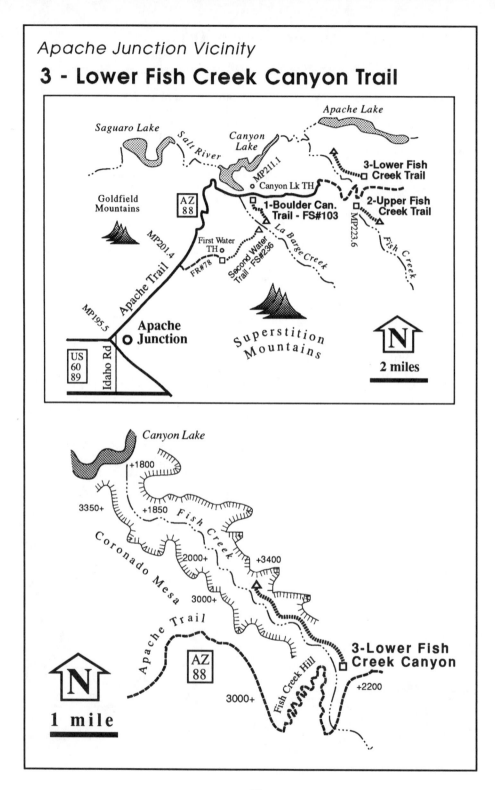

<u>3</u> - Fish Creek - Lower Canyon Trail

* Shallow water walk on primitive trail into deep, scenic canyon.

AZ 88 TH to creek pools
    2.0 mi; 200' loss

Special: Superstition Wilderness

Location: Apache Jct - 29 miles NE
Elevation: 2200'
Seasons: Dec - Mar
Agency: Tonto NF - Mesa RD
Topo map: Horse Mesa Dam

       Good transportation was critical to development of commerce on the frontier. In the 1880s it took a wagon two days to travel between Phoenix and Globe on a primitive road that is now the Apache Trail. Jack Frazier, a local rancher, ran a stage stop at lower Fish Creek Canyon. After 1900 the road was improved for transporting goods to Roosevelt Dam, reducing travel time to a day. In the 1940s, a paved two lane highway, US 60, was built south of the Superstitions, further reducing Phoenix-Globe travel time to a couple hours. The old stage stop on Apache Trail was converted to a campground, but a 1940s flood washed away the small camphouse, leaving only a small parking area as a reminder of pioneer days.

       If you hike down lower Fish Creek Canyon, you'll see near the road, among the weeds, the camphouse's concrete foundation along with a few steel anchors. Beyond that there is a primitive trail leading into the canyon. Although the hike is easy, it is not for novices, since some orienteering is required. The 1993 floods washed away the creekside trail and its canopy of cottonwoods and sycamores. So it is now a scenic water walk in the shallow creek. The canyon deepens further along the trail with saguaro dotting the upper slopes and fantastic formations carved out of the walls. A mile or two is a good day's effort, but don't consider hiking if rain is in the forecast - flash floods here are awesome.

       <u>**Directions to Trail Access**</u>**: From Apache Junction, at Apache Trail (AZ88) and Idaho Road, go NE 29 miles on AZ88 to the bottom of Fish Creek Hill. Go 0.8 miles more and park in a small lot on the north side of the road.**

Hiker relaxes in shade on wading adventure in Lower Fish Creek Canyon.

39

Area II. Globe Trails

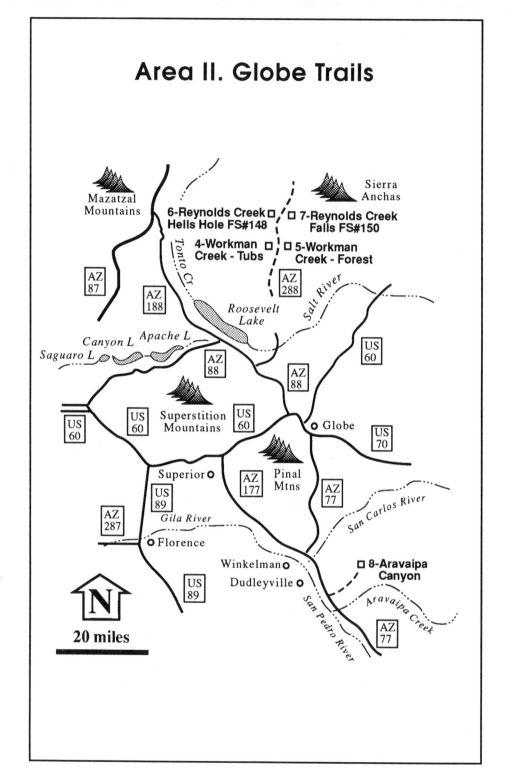

Mazatzal Mountains

Sierra Anchas

6-Reynolds Creek □ □ 7-Reynolds Creek
Hells Hole FS#148   Falls FS#150

4-Workman □ □ 5-Workman
Creek - Tubs   Creek - Forest

Tonto Cr.

AZ 87

AZ 188

AZ 288

Salt River

Roosevelt Lake

Canyon L   Apache L
Saguaro L

US 60

AZ 88

AZ 88

US 60

US 60   Superstition Mountains   US 60

Globe

US 70

US 60

Superior ○

AZ 177   Pinal Mtns

AZ 77

San Carlos River

US 89

Gila River

AZ 287

AZ 77

Florence ○

Winkelman ○
Dudleyville ○

□ 8-Aravaipa Canyon

Aravaipa Creek

US 89

San Pedro River

N

20 miles

Area II.
Globe Vicinity

HIKE DESCRIPTIONS & LOCAL MAPS

4 - Workman Creek - The Tubs Trail

5 - Workman Creek - Forest Trail

6 - Reynolds Creek - Hells Hole Trail FS#148

7 - Reynolds Creek - The Falls Trail FS#150

8 -Aravaipa Canyon Trail

Vertical rock walls shelter golden meadows on Aravaipa Canyon Trail.

4 - Workman Creek - Tubs Trail

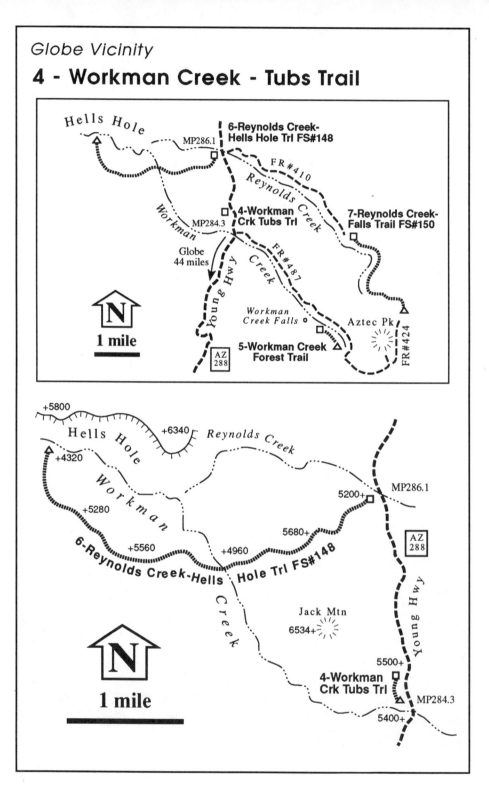

Hells Hole

MP286.1

**6-Reynolds Creek-
Hells Hole Trl FS#148**

FR#410

Reynolds Creek

**4-Workman
Crk Tubs Trl**

MP284.3

Workman

**7-Reynolds Creek-
Falls Trail FS#150**

Globe
44 miles

FR#487

Creek

Young Hwy

*Workman
Creek Falls*

Aztec Pk

FR#424

**5-Workman Creek
Forest Trail**

AZ
288

N

1 mile

+5800

Hells Hole

+6340

Reynolds Creek

+4320

Workman

5200+

MP286.1

+5280

AZ
288

6-Reynolds Creek-Hells

5680+

+5560

+4960

Hole Trl FS#148

Creek

Jack Mtn

6534+

Young Hwy

5500+

**4-Workman
Crk Tubs Trl**

MP284.3

5400+

N

1 mile

<u>4</u> - Workman Creek - The Tubs Trail

* A short steep hike down to small tiered waterfall splashing into pools.

AZ 88 to Workman Creek
    0.3 mi; 100' loss

Special: Sierra Ancha Wilderness

Location: Globe - 44 miles NW
Elevation: 5500'
Seasons: Apr - Oct
Agency: Tonto NF-Pleasant Vly RD
Topo map: Aztec Peak

    Was a frontier man's best friend his dog, his horse or, possibly, his mule? Place names often honored a pioneer's tragic incident, heroic deed, or homestead settlement, but Bill Lewis chose to remember his mule Jack. Bill was an early rancher in the Workman Creek area and occasionally called on Jack to pack goods from Globe, an arduous journey over difficult roads. Jack might have anticipated an upcoming trip, because he liked to temporarily escape his duties by heading up to his favorite hiding spot, the top of a mountain. Unfortunately, he always chose the same hideaway and was quickly found. But his independent character was rewarded with the namesake of the craggy, pine covered outcropping -- Jack Mountain.

    There is a short, primitive, quarter-mile trail just south of Jack Mountain and just north of the bridge over Workman Creek. It is a simple, but moderately steep, scramble down a pine covered slope to the creek. You can pause and taste some delicious fruit at a patch of blackberry bushes on the left hand side of the trail. At the creek there are a series of small waterfalls that cascade over gray-basalt boulders and splash into the stepped pools known as the Wash Tubs, or just The Tubs for short. The sun refracting off the ribbons of water make it a fine spot for picnicking or relaxing. It is a place that Bill and Jack may have once enjoyed.

    <u>**Directions to Trailhead**</u>: **From Globe, at AZ 88 and US 60, go northwest 18 miles on AZ 88 (MP258.2), turn right on AZ 288 (Globe-Young Hwy) and go north 26 miles (MP284.3). Pull off to the left just after Workman Creek Bridge and you'll see an opening that is usually signed as a hiking trail.**

Hiker snacks at minifalls at The Tubs along Workman Creek.

43

5 - Workman Creek - Forest Trail

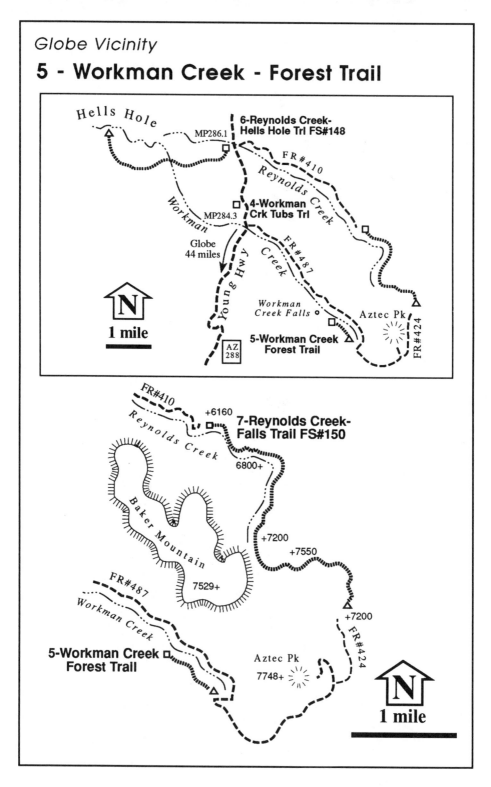

<u>5</u> - Workman Creek - Forest Trail

* Short, springtime hike by mossy rocks and forest stream near waterfall.

Waterfall to Spring	**Location:**	**Globe - 47 miles NW**
0.3 mi; 40' gain	**Elevation:**	**6400'**
	Seasons:	**Apr - Oct**
	Agency:	**Tonto NF-Pleasant Vly RD**
Special: Sierra Ancha Wilderness	**Topo map:**	**Aztec Peak**

The life of the everyday soldier on the frontier was not pleasant. The camps and forts were usually desolate and lonely places. Long stretches of interminable boredom were only occasionally punctuated by patrols with a real mortal danger. Food wasn't very good and pay was often in arrears. About a third of the enlisted men deserted. Yet, many of the soldiers stayed in Arizona after their terms had been served. Henry Wertman was a packer in the Union Army who, after his tour of duty, homesteaded a ranch at the base of Aztec Peak. The creek is named in his honor, but a mapmaker altered the spelling to Workman Creek.

There is a pleasant and easy hike along a short segment of the 10-mile-long Workman Creek that emerges from a spring by Aztec Peak. The primitive trail runs along a creek which flows through a cool, forested glen until it plunges 100' over a precipice at the forest's edge. This waterfall is a spectacular sight during snow melt in the spring, but is still a scenic, watery ribbon misting the mossy canyon walls in the summer. Casual hikers and picnickers can pull off the road above the waterfall and amble over to the creek for the short walk, but don't venture near the waterfall or cliff's edge, since this creek already has a name.

<u>Directions to Trail Access</u>: **From Globe, at AZ 88 & US 60, go northwest 18 miles on AZ 88 (MP258.2), turn right on AZ 288 (Globe-Young Hwy) and go north 26 miles (MP284.2), turn right on FS Rd#487 and go east 3.1 miles to the falls. The last mile after the gate is rough and restricted to high clearance vehicles. It is closed from November through March due to snow.**

Hikers enjoy splashing Workman Creek in Ponderosa pine forest.

6 - Hells Hole Trail FS#148

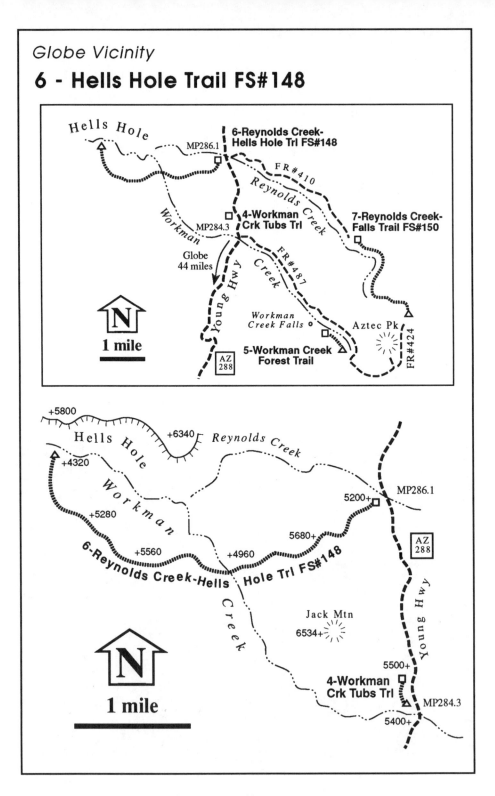

<u>6</u> - Reynolds Creek - Hells Hole Trail FS#148

A strenuous up and down trek to scenic creek in deep, rugged canyon.

FS Rd#487 TH to Hell's Hole
6 mi; 1500' gain

Special: Salome Creek Wilderness

Location:	Globe - 46 miles NW
Elevation:	5200'
Seasons:	Mar - May
Agency:	Tonto NF-Pleasant Vly RD
Maps:	Aztec Pk, Armer Mountain, Copper Mountain

In the 1870s and '80s tantalizing stories circulated around the ranges of Oklahoma and west Texas about an open land with waist-high grass, clear streams, and tall forests. These tales enticed many ranchers to move west to Arizona. One of the earliest pioneers was Colonel Jesse Ellison who, in 1885, brought 3000 head of cattle to Pleasant Valley. Among his range drivers were Glenn Reynolds and Bill McFadden. These two men, after seeing the opportunities that the rich land offered, returned to Texas, packed their families, and drove their own herds westward. They set up ranches at the southern end of Pleasant Valley by their namesakes, Reynolds Creek and McFadden Peak. The 15-mile-long creek descends rapidly from Aztec Peak, then winds its way down a deep, rocky canyon to its confluence with Workman Creek just upstream from the area called Hells Hole.

The hike starts by Reynolds Creek at the road and rises toward Jack Mountain. It then descends steeply to Workman Creek, goes over a high ridge, and finally drops steeply into Hells Hole. The canyon there is rugged, steep, and scenic, but the round trip hike has more than a 3000' net elevation gain and is recommended only for the well conditioned day hiker. The beautiful rolling meadows and verdant pine forest along the way explain why the land so appealed to the migrating Texans.

<u>Directions to Trailhead</u>: **From Globe, at AZ 88 and US 60, go northwest 18 miles on AZ 88 (MP258.2), turn right on to AZ 288 (Globe-Young Hwy) and go north 28 miles (MP286.1), turn left and park at the trailhead.**

Wildlife can sometimes be observed along Hells Hole trail.

7 - Reynolds Creek - Falls Trail FS#150

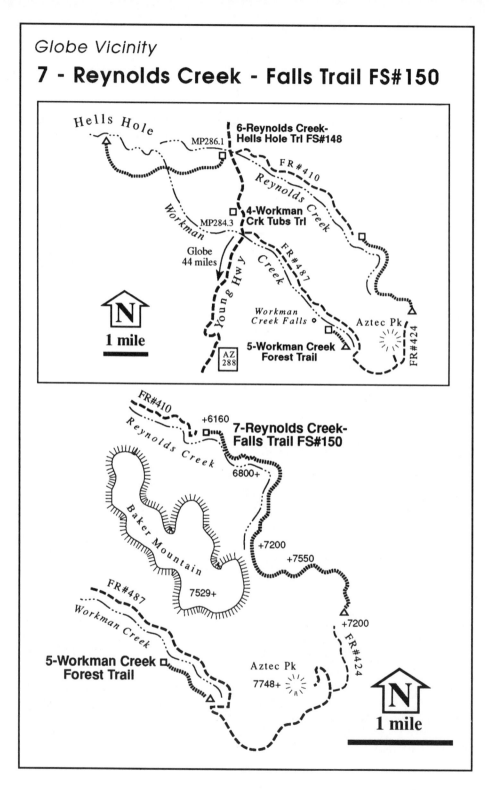

7 - Reynolds Creek Falls Trail FS#150

* A steep creek side hike to high falls and then into fir and aspen forest.

FS Rd#140 TH to Reynolds Falls	**Location:** Globe - 50 miles NW
0.8 mi; 300' gain	**Elevation:** 6160'
FS Rd#140 TH to Aztec Peak	**Seasons:** Apr - Oct
3.7 mi; 1040' gain	**Agency:** Tonto NF-Pleasant Vly RD
Special: Sierra Ancha Wilderness	**Topo map:** Aztec Peak

The wilderness stirred with war whoops, shouting, and the sound of shots echoing off a hill. After a brief struggle, sheriff Glen Reynolds and deputy Hunkydory Holmes lay dead and stage driver Gene Middleton lay wounded. On November 2, 1889 the lawmen were overpowered while escorting the "Apache Kid" and 7 other Indians from Globe to the railway station at Maricopa for the trip to Yuma prison. The Kid had been a reliable scout for the cavalry during the Geronimo campaign, but afterward had revenged his father's death by killing the guilty Apache. He was jailed, sent to trial, convicted of murder, and sentenced to a 7 year prison term.When the Kid sprung free he returned to the mountains and raided ranches, travelers, and reservations. He was never captured and his ultimate fate is still unknown.

The route on Reynolds Creek Trail from the trailhead to the 80' high waterfall is a short, but steep three-quarter mile-trek. Those without a high clearance vehicle can walk four miles (+1000' gain) up FS Rd#410 to the trailhead on a pleasant, but strenuous hike through the forest by the creek. Beyond the waterfall, the remainder of the trail ascends steeply through the pines to a cool, grassy plateau with stands of fir and aspen. The trail undulates along the plateau until it ends at a trailhead by Murphy Ranch near the top of Aztec Peak.

Directions to Trailhead: Starting in Globe, at AZ 88 and US 60, go NW 18 miles on AZ 88 (MP258.2), turn right on AZ 288 (Globe-Young Hwy) and go north 28 miles (MP286.1), turn right on FS Rd#410 and go north 4 miles to the trailhead. High clearance vehicles or walking are advised for this road.

A hiker finds a secluded spot in the forest along Reynolds Creek.

8 - Aravaipa Canyon Trail

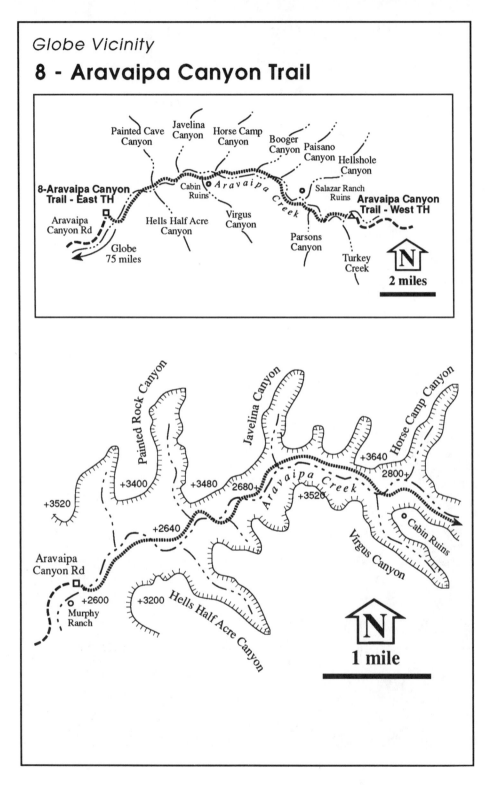

8 - Aravaipa Canyon Trail

* Easy walk by and through a shallow creek in wonderfully scenic canyon.

East TH to Old Cabin
    4.5 mi; 200' gain
East TH to West TH
    10.8mi; 440' gain
Special: Aravaipa Wilderness
    Permit Required

Location: Globe - 75 miles SE
Elevation: 2600'
Seasons: Apr - Oct
Agency: BLM Safford-357-7111
Maps: Brandenburg Mountain
      Booger Canyon

The Indians of Aravaipa Creek did not receive the safety and rations promised when they began to settle at Camp Grant near Tucson in 1870. But a few small bands of warriors from other tribes were still raiding homesteads south of the city. Citizen William S. Oury requested of territorial commander, General Stoneman, protection for the city, but was told that the 500 citizens could protect themselves. So on April 30, 1871 Oury, along with 98 Papagos, 48 Mexicans, and 5 whites, attacked the undefended reservation. Eight men and 104 women and children died. The Camp Grant Massacre outraged the nation, which led to Stoneman's removal and improved protection and benefits for Indians on reservations in the southwest.

One of the outstanding streamside hikes of central Arizona runs through the 11-mile-long riparian environs of Aravaipa Canyon. The 150 mile long Aravaipa Creek drains an extensive watershed and nourishes a broad diversity of species of plant and wildlife, many endangered, in the canyon. The trail runs along a flat plain a hundred yards wide with moderately easy walking along, across, and through the shallow, gravelly stream in the deep, colorful canyon. You might see here a deer, rattlers, and even a longhorn sheep or two.

Directions to Trailhead: From Globe, go east 3 mi on US 70, then south 60 mi on AZ 77 to Aravaipa Rd, and 12 mi east to the TH. (From Phoenix, go east 93 mi on US 60 to Superior, then 27 mi on AZ 177 to Winkelman, then south 12 mi on AZ 77 to Aravaipa Rd, and then 12 mi east to the TH.)

Hikers splash through lush riparian environment along Aravaipa Creek.

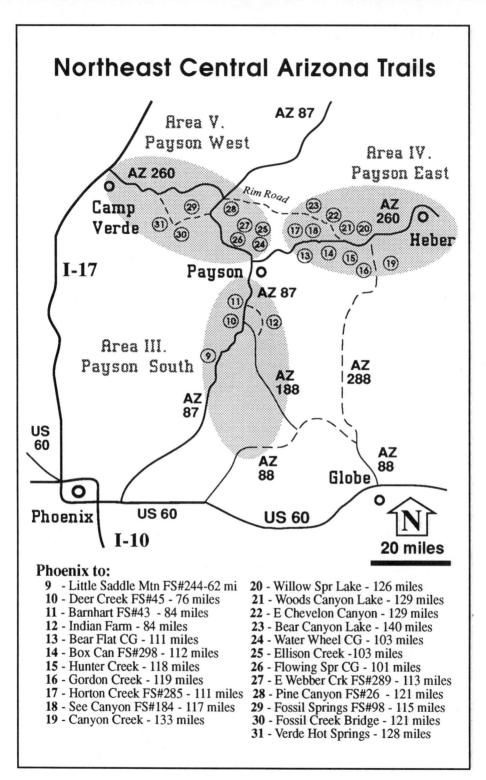

Northeast Central Arizona Trails

AZ 87

Area V.
Payson West

Area IV.
Payson East

AZ 260

Rim Road

Camp
Verde

AZ
260

Heber

I-17

Payson

AZ 87

Area III.
Payson South

AZ
188

AZ
288

AZ
87

US
60

AZ
88

AZ
88

Globe

Phoenix

US 60

US 60

I-10

N

20 miles

Phoenix to:
9 - Little Saddle Mtn FS#244-62 mi
10 - Deer Creek FS#45 - 76 miles
11 - Barnhart FS#43 - 84 miles
12 - Indian Farm - 84 miles
13 - Bear Flat CG - 111 miles
14 - Box Can FS#298 - 112 miles
15 - Hunter Creek - 118 miles
16 - Gordon Creek - 119 miles
17 - Horton Creek FS#285 - 111 miles
18 - See Canyon FS#184 - 117 miles
19 - Canyon Creek - 133 miles

20 - Willow Spr Lake - 126 miles
21 - Woods Canyon Lake - 129 miles
22 - E Chevelon Canyon - 129 miles
23 - Bear Canyon Lake - 140 miles
24 - Water Wheel CG - 103 miles
25 - Ellison Creek -103 miles
26 - Flowing Spr CG - 101 miles
27 - E Webber Crk FS#289 - 113 miles
28 - Pine Canyon FS#26 - 121 miles
29 - Fossil Springs FS#98 - 115 miles
30 - Fossil Creek Bridge - 121 miles
31 - Verde Hot Springs - 128 miles

Chapter 5. Northeast Central Arizona Trails

Area III. Payson South Vicinity
9 - Little Saddle Mtn Trail FS#244
10 - Deer Creek Trail FS#45
11 - Barnhart Trail FS#43
12 - Tonto Creek - Indian Farm Trail

Area IV. Payson East Vicinity
13 - Tonto Creek - Bear Flat CG Trail
14 - Christopher Crk - Box Can FS#298
15 - Hunter Creek Trail
16 - Gordon Creek Trail
17 - Horton Creek Trail FS#285
18 - Christopher Crk - See Can FS#184
19 - Canyon Creek Trail
20 - Willow Springs Lake Trail
21 - Woods Canyon Lake Trail
22 - East Chevelon Creek Trail
23 - Bear Canyon Lake Trail

Area V. Payson West Vicinity
24 - East Verde River - Water Wheel CG Trl
25 - Ellison Creek Trail
26 - East Verde River - Flowing Spr CG Trail
27 - East Webber Creek Trail FS#289
28 - Pine Canyon Trail FS#26
29 - Fossil Springs Trail FS#98
30 - Fossil Creek - Bridge Trail
31 - Verde River - Verde Hot Springs Trail

Hiker surveys rugged terrain of Christorpher Creek along Box Canyon.

Area III. Payson South Trails

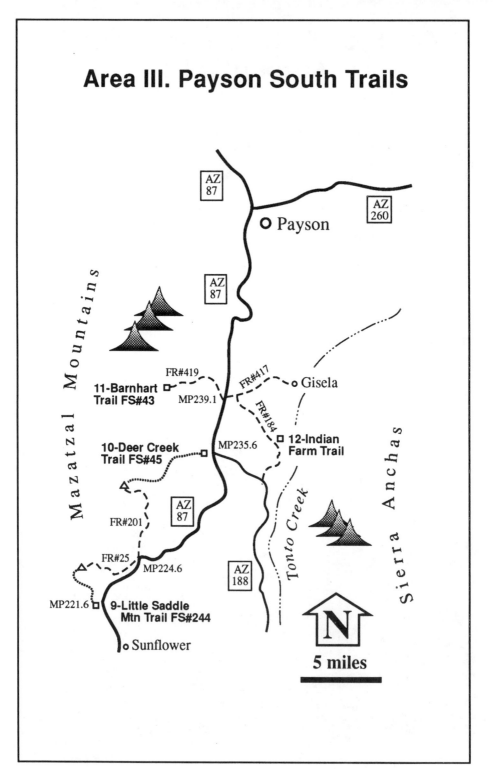

AZ 87

Payson

AZ 260

Mazatzal Mountains

AZ 87

FR#419

FR#417

Gisela

11-Barnhart
Trail FS#43

MP239.1

FR#184

10-Deer Creek
Trail FS#45

MP235.6

12-Indian
Farm Trail

Sierra Anchas

AZ 87

FR#201

Tonto Creek

FR#25

MP224.6

AZ 188

MP221.6

9-Little Saddle
Mtn Trail FS#244

Sunflower

N

5 miles

Area III.
Payson South Vicinity

HIKE DESCRIPTIONS & LOCAL MAPS

9 - Little Saddle Mountain Trail #244

10 - Deer Creek Trail FS#45

11 - Barnhart Trail FS#43

12 - Tonto Creek - Indian Farm Trail

Spring storm drifting in replenishes creek along Barnhart Trail.

9 - Little Saddle Mountain Trail FS#244

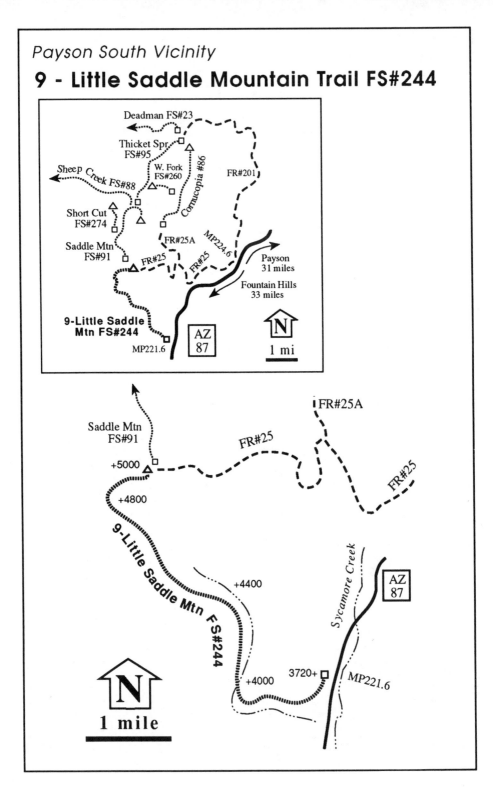

Deadman FS#23

Thicket Spr.
FS#95

Sheep Creek FS#88

W. Fork
FS#260

Cornucopia #86

FR#201

Short Cut
FS#274

Saddle Mtn
FS#91

FR#25A

MP224.6

FR#25

FR#25

Payson
31 miles

Fountain Hills
33 miles

**9-Little Saddle
Mtn FS#244**

MP221.6

AZ
87

N

1 mi

Saddle Mtn
FS#91

FR#25A

FR#25

FR#25

+5000

+4800

9-Little Saddle Mtn FS#244

+4400

Sycamore Creek

AZ
87

+4000

3720+

MP221.6

N

1 mile

<u>9</u> - Little Saddle Mountain Trail FS#244

* Moderate uphill hike by a spring fed creek to cascade and small pool.

Trailhead to Cascade
    2.0 mi; 600' gain
Trailhead to Trail End
    4.5 mi; 1320' gain
Special: Mazatzal Wilderness

Location: Payson - 31 miles S
Elevation: 3720'
Seasons: Mar - May, Sep - Nov
Agency: Tonto NF - Mesa RD
Maps: Reno Pass, Lion Mountain

How was it that Vincent Colyer, New York artist and member of the Academy of Design, came to be called a "treacherous, black-hearted dog" by Arizona newspapers? As Secretary of the Board of Indians, he visited many Indian villages in 1871, with the authority to choose reservation sites. His selections (including Camps Apache, Verde, and McDowell) were mostly approved in Washington. But Colyer was vilified by the local citizenry because the designation of reservations would put an end to seizure by whites of Indian lands with valuable mineral, ranching, and agricultural resources. Today, he is recognized for helping to bring peace to the southwest by setting up the reservation system much as it now exists.

On the Little Saddle Mountain Trail you'll see Sunflower Valley just to the south, where an important conference was held between Colyer and Chief Shelter Pau on October 1, 1871. The hike's first mile is a delight in the spring, with pinyon and juniper shading a sparkling stream decorated with yellow columbine, red penstemon, and white agave blossoms. The next mile is steeper and more exposed, but shows off lava-capped peaks soaring from deep gorges. Off to the north, before the two-mile point, a ten-foot-high waterfall trickles into a shallow pool. Two miles beyond are fine views of the Mazatzals to the south and the west.

<u>Directions to Trailhead</u>: Starting in Payson, at AZ 87 and AZ 260, go south 31 miles on AZ 87 to MP221.6 (or, from Fountain Hills, at Shea Blvd. and AZ 87, go north 33 miles on AZ 87). Park in the small lot on east side of road. Cross the road and climb a shallow grade to the trailhead.

Hikers cool their feet in minipool on Little Saddle Mountain Trail.

10 - Deer Creek Trail FS#45

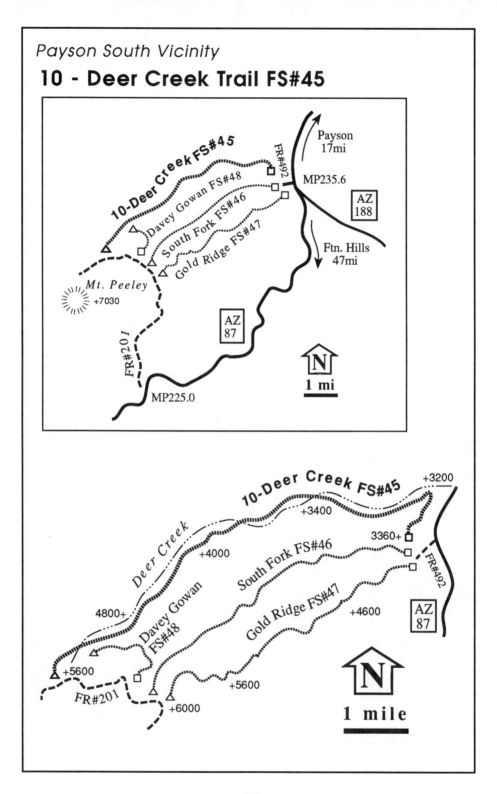

<u>10</u> - Deer Creek Trail FS#45

* Moderately hilly hike by springtime creek in pine forest canyon.

Trailhead to Gowan Grave	**Location:**	**Payson - 17 miles S**
2.5 mi; 200' gain	**Elevation:**	**3360'**
Trailhead to Mt. Peeley Summit	**Seasons:**	**Mar - May**
9.5 mi; 2240' gain	**Agency:**	**Tonto NF-Tonto Basin RD**
Special: Mazatzal Wilderness	**Maps:**	**Mazatzal Peak, Gisela**

The seemingly unlimited land of the American West offered great opportunities for the land-poor European immigrants. One was Scotsman Davey Gowan, who homesteaded land by Gisela in 1874. The territory was still dangerous then, as evidenced by the fact that his partner had to watch for Indians while he dug an orchard irrigation ditch. Later, Gowan heard of Tonto Natural Bridge, the world's largest limestone arch. He went there in 1881 to develop it as a tourist site, but later gave it to relatives from Scotland. Finally, in 1916, he built a cabin on Deer Creek and tended a garden and an orchard while working local mining claims.

On this hike you can become intimately acquainted with Gowan's Deer Creek, which runs 10 miles from Mt. Peeley into Rye Creek. It flows most of the year, but is best in the spring when charged with melting winter snows. The trail starts by traversing cross country a half-mile to the creek where you'll begin walking under cottonwoods and sycamores. It then rolls up and down the hills next to the creek through a semi-shaded forest of pine and live oak. You can stop after a few hours of hiking or climb the tough nine miles to the summit. But keep your eyes open for a small clearing at two-and-a-half miles. A small gravestone marks the spot where 83-year-old Davey Gowan was reunited with the land he loved.

<u>**Directions to Trailhead**</u>**: Starting from Payson, at AZ 87 and AZ 260, go south 17 miles on AZ 87 to MP235.6 (or, from Fountain Hills, at Shea Blvd. & AZ 87, go north 47 miles on AZ 87), turn west on to FS Rd #492 and go 0.5 miles to trailhead. Follow the Deer Creek FS#45 signs to the north.**

Winter runoff cascades over and around boulders in Deer Creek.

11 - Barnhart Trail FS#43

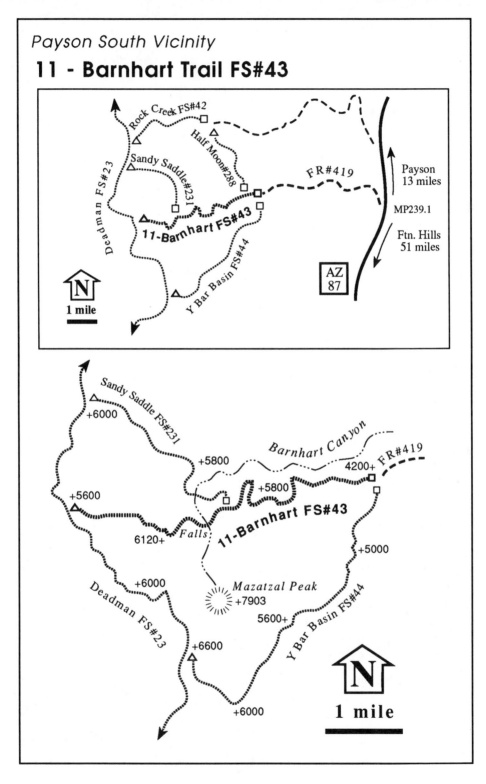

<u>11</u> - Barnhart Trail FS#43

* Moderately steep hike near springtime creek to surprise 50' waterfall.

FS Rd#419 TH to Waterfall	Location: Payson - 17 miles S
3.3 mi; 1600' gain	Elevation: 4200'
FS Rd#419 TH to Overlook	Seasons: Mar - Apr
6.1 mi; 1920' gain	Agency: Tonto NF - Payson RD
Special: Mazatzal Wilderness	Maps: Barnhart Can, Mazatzal Pk

Boom and bust mining towns sprang up regularly around Arizona, and one such settlement that came to life in the Mazatzals was Marysville. It was named after Mary Margaret Chilson whose father, Emer, built a general store for the mining camp located four miles southwest of Payson. As the town's population grew to 300, the store prospered, and typical 1881 values included; 25c/lb for honey, 30c/lb for coffee, 20c/lb for mule shoes, and $17/oz for gold. But the area's claims were shallow and played out within a half dozen years, after which the store and the town were abandoned. The rewards for mining in the area have been summed up by a phrase from the book *Rim Country History*, which quotes an old-timer, "Payson mines are like teases -- they show you enough to lead you on, but never produce."

The Barnhart Trailhead, which sits a dozen miles south of the Marysville site, will give you a feeling of the parched, chaparral-and-scrub environment that the early miners endured. But there is more to the trail than just scrub. The first mile of the trail rises above a splashing spring time creek that runs through a deep canyon. The trail then steepens and displays fine views of the eastern Verde Valley, Payson, and the Mogollon Rim. And after three miles there's a 50'-high springtime waterfall tumbling down a chute off the south side of the trail. Another three miles leads to the trail's end with panoramic views of the western Mazatzals.

<u>**Directions to Trailhead**</u>: **From Payson, at AZ 87 and AZ 260, go south 13 miles on AZ 87 to MP239.1 (or, from Fountain Hills, at Shea Blvd. & AZ 87, go north 51 miles on AZ 87). Go west 4 miles on FS Rd#419 to trailhead.**

Fifty-foot waterfall springs to life in late March during snow melt.

12 - Indian Farm Trail

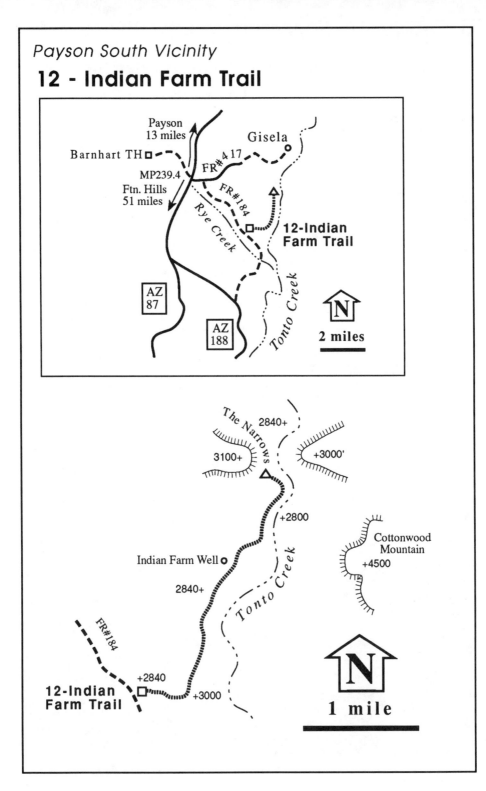

12 - Tonto Creek - Indian Farm Trail

* Hike over hill to vista of Tonto Basin and visit Tonto Creek Narrows.

FS Rd#184 TH to Indian Farm   Location: Payson - 17 miles S
      2.0 mi; 160' gain + 160' loss   Elevation: 2840'
FS Rd#184 TH to Tonto Creek   Seasons: Sep - Nov
      3.0 mi; 160' gain + 200' loss   Agency: Tonto NF-Tonto Basin RD
Special: Wildlife - Closed 12/1-6/30   Topo map: Gisela

Government policies towards Indians on the frontier in the 1860s and 70s often did not reward compliance with the benefits proposed. Many natives relinquished claim to their rich, ancestral lands with the promise of cattle, grain, and farming land on a reservation. That land was frequently barren and difficult to till and deliveries of goods were sporadic. Occasionally, settlers allowed some natives to forage an existence on plots of off-reservation land. One such plot was Indian Farm near Gisela. Slim Ellison, who lived in the area as a teenager, tells of the Indians' meals of boiled and skinned pack rats and of vegetable broths from the boiling of local greens. Unfortunately, their lot was better than many of their kin on the reservations.

The trail to Indian Farm and Tonto Creek leads over a moderate rise into the Tonto Basin. It follows an old jeep road to a working windmill and cattle tank. There is half mile walk down to the creek which is not for novices, since bushwhacking and pathfinding are required. A half mile north are the scenic Narrows, with possibilities for picnicking or swimming. Fall is the best time to hike since the trail is closed December through June. It is a pleasant enough area to visit, but you wouldn't want to have to eke out an existence there.

<u>Directions to Trail Access</u>: From Payson, at AZ 87 and AZ 260, go south 13 miles on AZ 87 to MP239.4 (or, from Fountain Hills, at Shea Blvd. & AZ 87, go north 51 miles on AZ 87), turn east on FS Rd#417 (to Gisela) and go 0.2 miles. Turn right and go south 3.8 miles on FS Rd#184 to a narrow jeep road, FS Rd#3414, on the east which is the unmarked point of trail access.

Hikers pause by working windmill at Indian Farm en route to Tonto Creek.

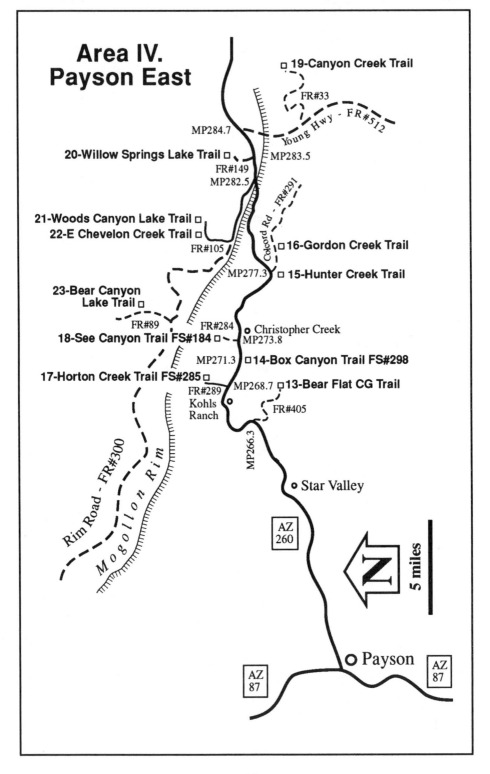

Area IV.
Payson East

□ **19-Canyon Creek Trail**

FR#33

Young Hwy - FR#512

MP284.7

20-Willow Springs Lake Trail □

MP283.5

FR#149

MP282.5

Colcord Rd - FR#291

21-Woods Canyon Lake Trail □

22-E Chevelon Creek Trail □

□ **16-Gordon Creek Trail**

FR#105

MP277.3

□ **15-Hunter Creek Trail**

**23-Bear Canyon
Lake Trail** □

FR#89

FR#284

18-See Canyon Trail FS#184 □

Christopher Creek

MP273.8

MP271.3

□ **14-Box Canyon Trail FS#298**

17-Horton Creek Trail FS#285 □

MP268.7 □ **13-Bear Flat CG Trail**

FR#289
Kohls
Ranch

FR#405

MP266.3

Rim Road - FR#300

Mogollon Rim

Star Valley

AZ
260

N

5 miles

Payson

AZ
87

AZ
87

Area IV.
Payson East Vicinity

HIKE DESCRIPTIONS & LOCAL MAPS

13 - Tonto Creek - Bear Flat Campground Trail

14 - Christopher Creek - Box Canyon Trail FS#298

15 - Hunter Creek Trail

16 - Gordon Creek Trail

17 - Horton Creek Trail FS#285

18 - Christopher Creek - See Canyon Trail FS#184

19 - Canyon Creek Trail

20 - Willow Springs Lake Trail

21 - Woods Canyon Lake Trail

22 - East Chevelon Creek Trail

23 - Bear Canyon Lake Trail

East Chevelon Creek carves a serpentine path down forested meadow.

13 - Bear Flat Campground Trail

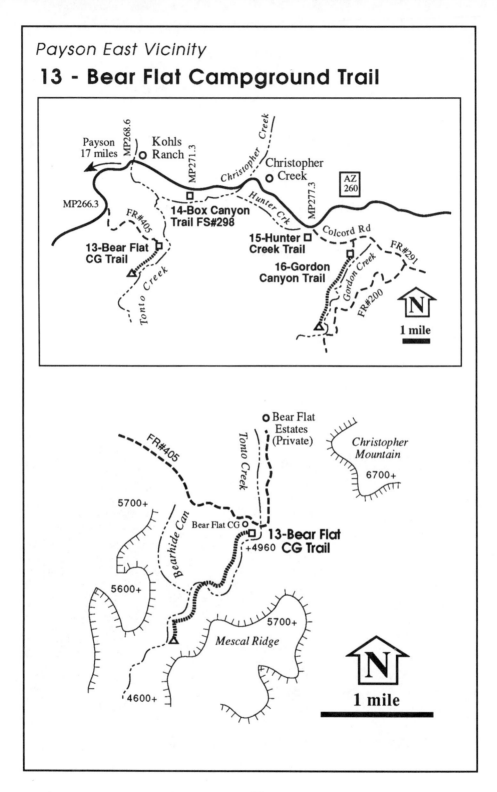

<u>13</u> - Tonto Creek - Bear Flat Campground Trail

* Primitive route with creek wading, bushwhacking, & boulder clambering.

Bear Flat CG to Creek Pools
    0.4 mi; 20' loss
Bear Flat CG to Canyon Narrows
    1.5 mi; 100' loss
Special: Hellsgate Wilderness

Location: Payson - 18 miles E
Elevation: 4960'
Seasons: May - Oct
Agency: Tonto NF - Payson RD
Topo map: Promontory Butte

A muted jangle from the shadows, a shot, and another rattler lay motionless. Slim Ellison told a story where he, as a young boy traveling with his family at the turn of the century, had camped in Hellsgate, a rugged canyon at the confluence of Haigler and Tonto Creeks. The campsite was plagued with rattlers and the warmth of the campfire attracted the cold blooded creatures after dusk. So his father surrounded the area with a low wire mesh. At the sound of a rattle he'd raise a kerosene lamp and dispatch the snake with his six gun. Today, the wonder of our wilderness areas is that the same dangers, beauty, and isolation still exist, much as they had a century ago.

The Hellsgate Wilderness' northern tip may be accessed from Bear Flat Campground. There is a primitive fisherman's path that runs south a half mile and jogs back and forth across Tonto Creek. Wear water shoes and be prepared to test your bushwhacking and boulder clambering skills. The scenery is spectacular, with canyon walls that soar upward a thousand feet and deep pools that invite fishing or swimming. Beyond a half mile the path becomes even more difficult and is recommended only for experienced trekkers. Besides rattlers, another danger still present here is the threat of flash floods. Water funneling into the deep canyon can raise the creek's level 10' to 20', so avoid the area if rain is in the forecast.

<u>**Directions to Trail Access**</u>**: From Payson, at AZ 87 and AZ 260, go east 14 miles on AZ 260 (MP266.3), turn right and go S 1.3 miles on FS Rd#405, turn left and go another 3.0 miles on FS Rd#405 to Bear Flat CG and park.**

Trekkers wade across Tonto Creek on hike down rugged canyon.

14 - Box Canyon Trail FS#298

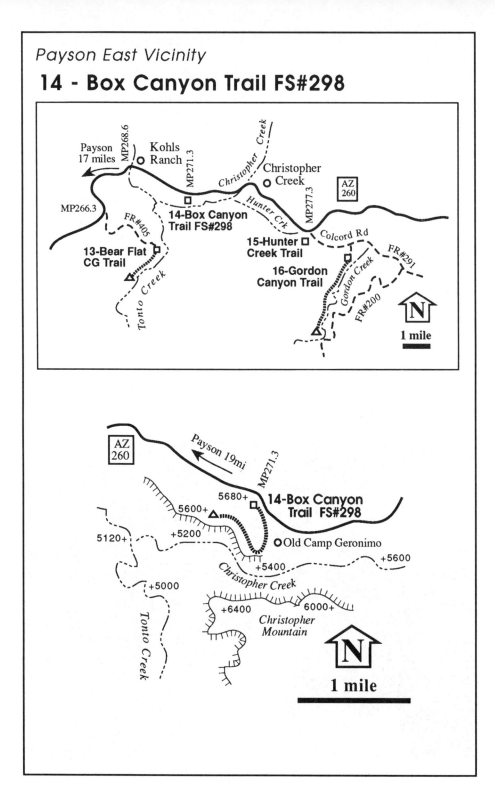

<u>14</u> - Christopher Creek - Box Canyon Trail FS#298

* Nice walk to creek cascading through a deep, chiseled basalt canyon.

AZ 260 TH to Christopher Creek 0.6 mi; 280' loss	Location:	Payson - 19 miles E
	Elevation:	5680'
	Seasons:	May - Oct
	Agency:	Tonto NF - Payson RD
	Topo map:	Promontory Butte

Frontier towns usually had a few important families that helped settle the area and develop the community. The Haught family, which homesteaded places east of Payson, was one of those. Fred, a former Texas ranger, was the first to arrive. As a prospector in Cripple Creek, Colorado, he helped save a greenhorn's life by gunning down three ruffians. To preserve his health he fled and ended up homesteading in Pleasant Valley. He told family about the wonderful land and "Babe" Haught came up from Texas to homestead by the head of Tonto Creek. Babe raised cattle and became a guide for Zane Grey, eventually selling him 3 acres of land for a hunting lodge. Babe's son, Edd, worked with the local youth as a scoutmaster and developed homesteaded land on Christopher Creek into old Camp Geronimo for the Boy Scouts. It still stands today as a remembrance of his civic generosity.

The Box Canyon Trail runs southeast across and down through the Ponderosas to Christopher Creek. On the way, as the trail skirts the camp boundary, you'll see some old wooden scout dorms. At the creek you can walk up the north bank for a fine view of the dramatic cascades and pools at the bottom of the deep canyon. Or you can bring your swimming trunks and wade into the clear, cool, refreshing pools (be careful, they're slippery) where you might even end up sharing the water with a few scouts from Haught's old camp.

Directions to the Trailhead: From Payson, at AZ 87 and AZ 260, go east 19 miles on AZ 260 (MP271.3) and turn right into the lot. From the trailhead head southeast to pick up the path that leads down to the creek.

Hiker beats the heat in cool pools of Box Canyon on Christopher Creek.

15 - Hunter Creek Trail

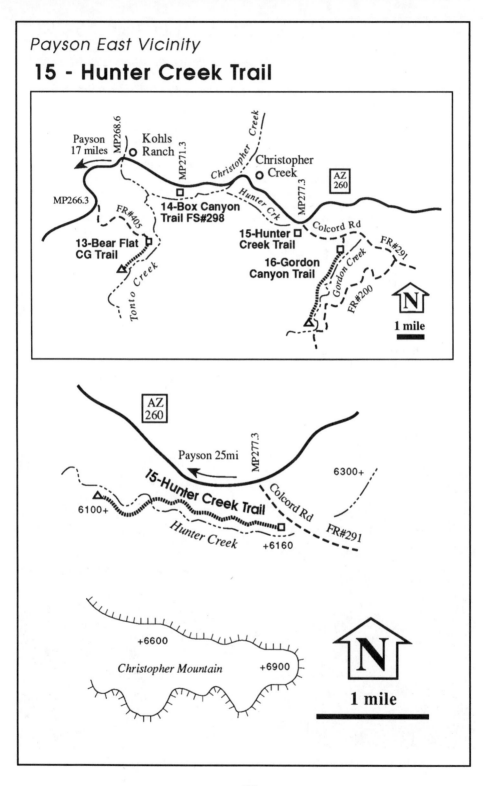

<u>15</u> - Hunter Creek Trail

* Primitive, easy walk through meadow and forest by bubbling brook.

FS Rd #291 to Forest Area
    2.5 mi; 60' loss

Location: Payson - 25 miles E
Elevation: 6160'
Seasons: May - Oct
Agency: Tonto NF - Payson RD
Topo map: Woods Canyon

    Early pioneer roads developed from old Indian trails that usually followed creek beds and land contours. Until the turn of the century, there was a tortuous route from Payson to Pleasant Valley. It first followed rolling hills through Star Valley and Greenback Valley out to Kohl's Ranch. It then moved down Tonto Creek, up over a rise to Christopher Creek, east along Hunter Creek, and finally cross country to Canyon Creek in Pleasant Valley. This was also the route followed by a band of four dozen Indian warriors from Cibique Creek. They went on the warpath when the military unjustly arrested and killed a young medicine man at a conference on August 30, 1881. In revenge, they burned, looted, and killed for almost a year until they were defeated at the Battle of Big Dry Wash on the Mogollon Rim on July 17, 1882.

    You'll be able to view part of the route used by the pioneers and the Indians when you hike through the meadows and woods along Hunter Creek. It is a beautiful walk for two or three miles, first through waist high grass, and then along a shady path under Ponderosa pines. A number of cascades trickle off slabs of red rocks into shallow pools filled with craw dads. Head back if you see a bull and cattle grazing by the creek. But other than that, hike as far as you want, soaking up the sun, scenery, and history of the area.

    <u>**Directions to Trail Access**</u>**: From Payson, at AZ 87 and AZ 260, go east 25 miles on AZ 260 to Colcord Road-FS Rd#291 (MP277.3). Turn right and go 0.3 miles and park at an unmarked road. Walk 30 yards west, go through the gate and follow the creek through the meadow and beyond.**

Small cascades pour into crawdad filled pools along Hunter Creek.

16 - Gordon Creek Trail

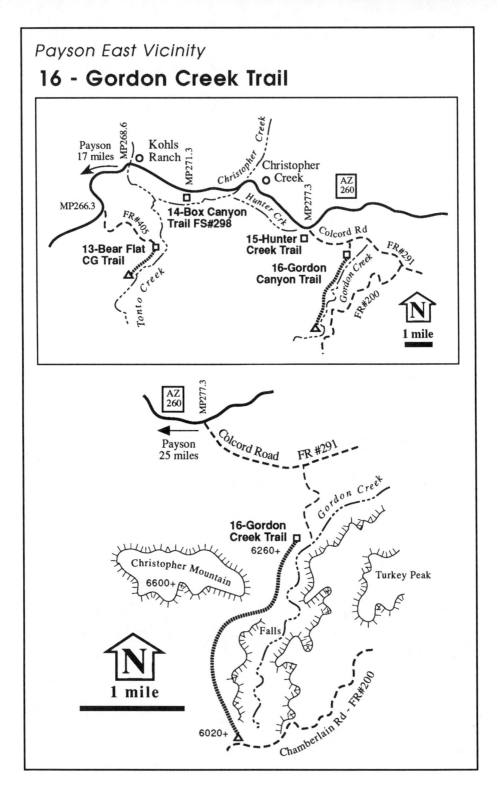

<u>16</u> - Gordon Creek Trail - FS#180

* Walk in forest, then along rocky creek bank to twenty-foot falls and pool.

FS Rd#291 to Creek
    1.2 mi; 50' loss
FS Rd#291 to Falls
    2.5 mi; 100' loss

Location: Payson - 26 miles E
Elevation: 6260'
Seasons: May - Oct
Agency: Tonto NF - Payson RD
Maps: Woods Canyon, Oxbow Mtn

      Education was important to the pioneers, but sparse populations, rough terrain, and children's ranch responsibilities made the task of schooling difficult. A county in Arizona Territory would support a teacher for a school as long as there were at least eight students available for instruction. One of the earliest, though shortest-lived, schools in Pleasant Valley was the old log cabin near Gordon Creek at the bottom of Turkey Mountain. For a little while, in the early 1900s, there were enough kids on homesteads by Gordon Creek and Haigler Creek to support a school. An old-timer, Vern Gillette, has recalled the bonds built from the fun, the learning, and the sense of community that developed at the school.

      A portion of this hike once took kids to school almost a century ago, but today you'll need pathfinding skills to stay on the right jeep trail. From Colcord Road an unmarked road runs southeast a mile until it intersects Gordon Creek. From here the trail jogs back and forth across the creek for a mile and then circles southwest around a rugged, rocky area along the creek. Experienced hikers can rock scramble a half mile along the creek to the scenic Falls, a 25' waterfall that splashes into a deep pool. Otherwise you can follow the jeep trail another two miles to where it intersects with Gordon Creek again at Chamberlain Road.

      <u>Directions to Trail Access</u>: **From Payson, at AZ 87 and AZ 260, go east 25 miles on AZ 260 to Colcord Road-FS Rd#291 (MP277.3). Turn right and go southeast 1.3 miles, just 40 yards S of the power lines, and park at the unmarked road. Walk or drive a high clearance vehicle a mile to the creek.**

Scenic falls reward hikers' efforts on Gordon Creek Canyon Trail.

17 - Horton Creek Trail FS#285

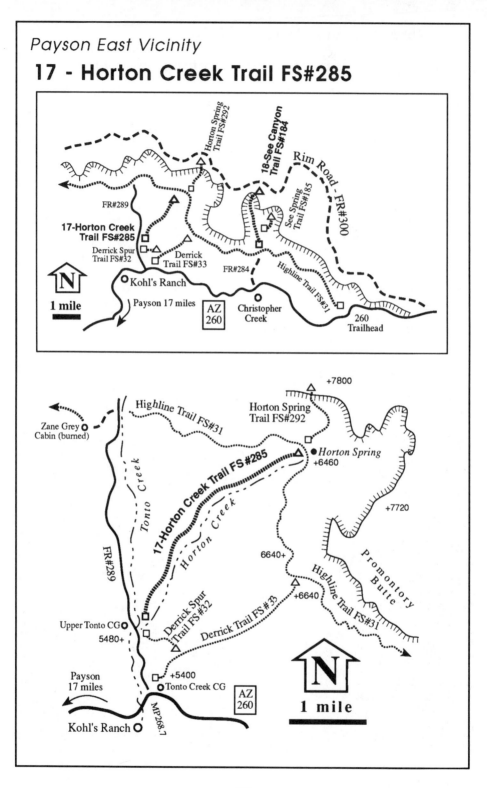

17 - Horton Creek Trail FS#285

* Moderate climb in pine forest to mountainside spring gushing into pool.

Tonto CG TH to Horton Spring
     3.8 mi; 980' gain
Tonto CG TH to to Rim
     4.7 mi; 2320' gain
	Location: Payson - 18 miles E
	Elevation: 5480'
	Seasons: May - Oct
	Agency: Tonto NF-Payson Dist.
	Topo map: Promontory Butte

"Then she heard strange wild yelps, stacatto, piercing, somehow infinitely lonely. They made her shudder. 'Coyotes' said Glenn." So is described the eerie atmosphere in Zane Grey's classic western novel, *To the Last Man*. The rough life and hard times in Arizona Territory were much romanticized in dime novels and later in Hollywood movies. The most famous writer was Zane Grey, former New York dentist and semipro ball player, whose sense of adventure drew him to Arizona. His famous "Last Man" novel was a semifictional account of the tragic 1890s war between the Tewkesberry and Graham clans which claimed 29 lives. It was set in the rugged terrain of Pleasant Valley just 15 miles east of Grey's hunting lodge.

The Horton Creek Trail lies three miles east of Grey's lodge and gives a taste of the inspiring landscapes in his novel. The route begins at the bridge and follows an old jeep trail on the west side of the dry creek bed up through a pine forest. After a mile, the creek springs to life and you'll see some nice cascades at intervals along the path. After four miles, the base of the Mogollon Rim looms ahead. Go 100 yards east to where Horton Spring splashes from the mountainside down mossy rocks into a large shallow pool. Or go a bit further and head up the steep, strenuous, 1000'-high Horton Springs Trail for a classic Zane Grey panorama.

Directions to Trailhead: **From Payson, at AZ 87 and AZ 260, go 17 miles east on AZ 260 (MP268.7), just past Kohl's Ranch. Turn left on FS Rd#289, go N 1.5 miles and turn left into the Tonto CG lot. Walk east across the road and bridge and then cross down to the west side of the dry creek to the trail.**

Hiker takes a break to cool hot feet along Horton Creek Trail.

18 - See Canyon Trail FS#184

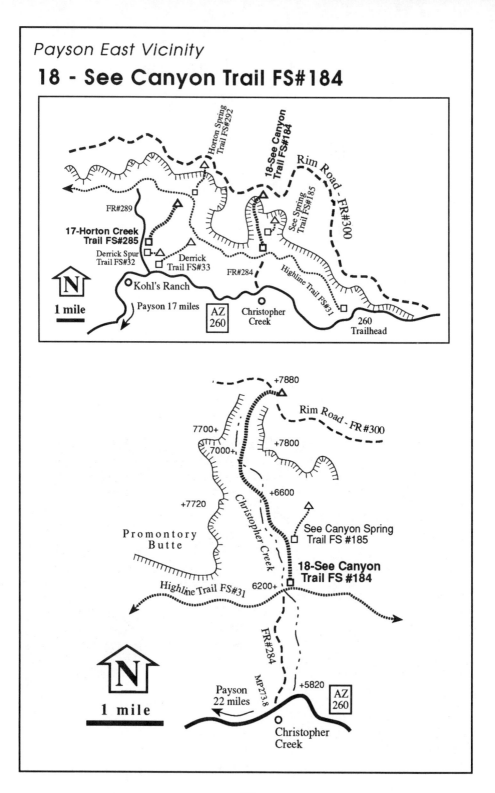

<u>18</u> - Christopher Creek - See Canyon Trail FS#184

* Uphill climb in pine & maple forest along rocky, springtime creek.

AZ 260 to Trailhead
    1.5 mi; 380' gain
AZ 260 to Rim
    4.7 mi; 2060' gain
	Location: Payson - 24 miles E
	Elevation: 5820'
	Seasons: May - Oct
	Agency: Tonto NF - Payson RD
	Topo map: Promontory Butte

      The troops noticed a pungent, piny odor and, after moving further ahead, saw wisps of bluish-gray smoke floating up from the brittle, black ashes. Full rites and interment were performed on the charred remains found inside the burned cabin. Only later did the soldiers curiously discover that the bones were those from the body of a bear that homesteader Isadora Christopher had just hung inside his cabin before departing on a trip. He was a lucky one on that day in July, 1882, since a half dozen settlers had already been killed by the four-dozen Cibique Indians who were on the warpath. The warriors were later defeated at the Battle of Big Dry Wash and the nearby stream became the Frenchman's namesake, Christopher Creek.

      The See Canyon Trail runs next to and across the upper portion of Christopher Creek, which dries up in the summer. It is a moderate, then steep, trek up to the Rim. The forest obscures the Rim panorama, but there are some nice red rock grottoes and ancient 500-year-old alligator junipers along the way. The scenery is best either in the spring, when snow melt cascades down the creek, or in autumn, when the pine forest lights up with scattered stands of iridescent pink maples and brilliant yellow oaks. If there's time, you might also try the short See Canyon Spring Trail which leads to a beautiful meadow of waist-high golden grass.

      <u>Directions to Trailhead</u>: **From Payson, at AZ 87 and AZ 260, go 22 miles east on AZ 260 (MP273.8) into the town of Christopher Creek. Go 1.5 miles north up FS Rd#284 to the trailhead with a high clearance vehicle, or, park on the south side of AZ 260 and walk up to the trailhead.**

Hikers enjoy brilliant fall colors on See Canyon Trail by Christopher Creek.

19-Canyon Creek Trail

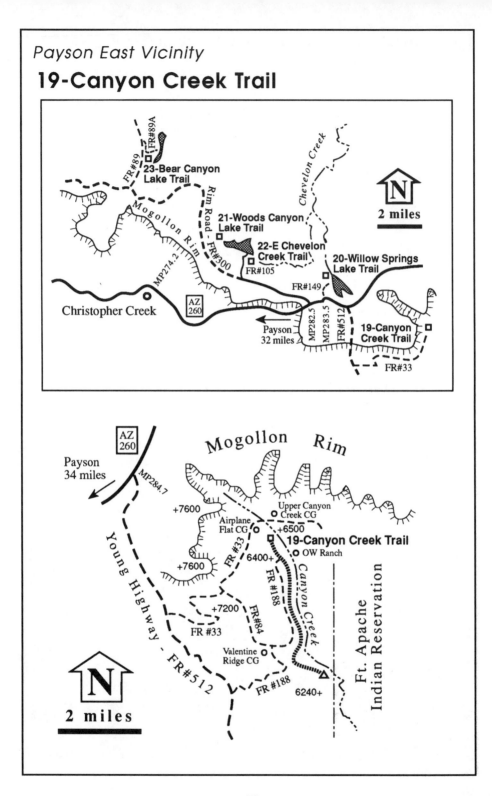

<u>19</u> - Canyon Creek Trail

* Crisscross creek walk on fisherman's trail through meadow and canyon.

Airplane Flat CG to Reservation Bdy	**Location:**	**Payson - 40 miles E**
5.0 mi; 260' loss	**Elevation:**	**6500'**
	Seasons:	**May - Oct**
	Agency:	**Tonto NF-Pleasant Vly RD**
	Maps:	**OW Point, Parallel Canyon**

On September 1, 1887, sheriff Commodore Perry Owens served a warrant for horse rustling to Andy Blevins at the family home in Holbrook. Within a minute, two men lay dead, one dying, and another wounded. Owens was untouched. It was the bloodiest incident in the the violent Pleasant Valley War, which claimed 29 lives in 15 years. In Arizona Territory the rugged terrain, the remote ranches, and long travel times often meant that the law was what you made of it. An argument between the Tewkesberrys and the Grahams turned into a war where everyone took sides (Blevins supported the Grahams). Now the quiet meadows and forests belie the violence that stirred the land long ago and is still whispered about today.

The hike follows Canyon Creek down an unmarked fisherman's path that heads south, crossing the water many times. It requires some pathfinding experience and you'll probably get your feet wet. You'll see OW Ranch (owned by Blevins?) two miles down from the Rim and in late summer you'll pass broad, golden meadows aglow with a rainbow of wildflowers. Further along, the creek wanders into a grayish, basaltic canyon whose walls are tiered, fractured and covered with light green and deep black lichen. Finally, the public path terminates in a slabbed red rock canyon at the Fort Apache Reservation Boundary.

<u>**Directions to Trail Access**</u>**: From Payson, at AZ 87 and AZ 260, go east 32 miles on AZ 260 (MP284.7), turn right on Young Rd-FS Rd#512 and go south 3 miles to Canyon Creek Rec Area Rd-FS#33. Turn left and go east 5 miles to Airplane Flat CG. Follow fisherman's path through bushes to creek.**

Hikers congratulate themselves on dry crossing of Canyon Creek.

20-Willow Springs Lake Trail

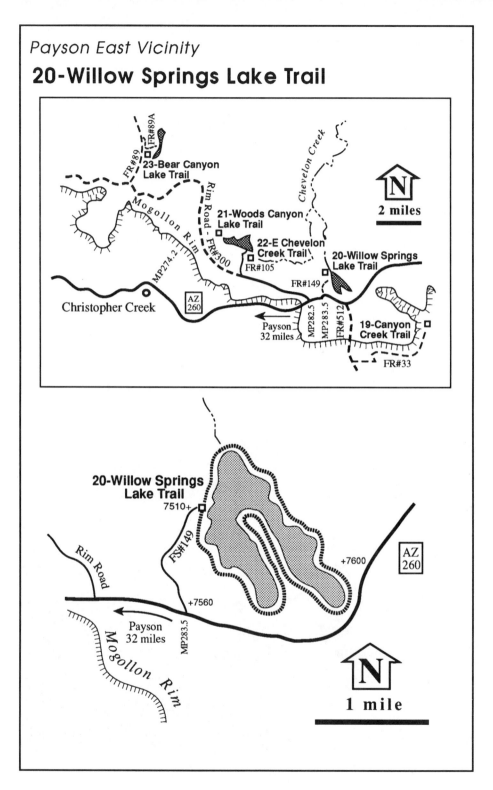

<u>20</u> - Willow Springs Lake Trail

* Pleasant forest walk on dirt and rock fisherman's trail around lake.

Parking Area Lake Loop
    3.5 mi; 60' gain

Location:	Payson - 33 miles E
Elevation:	7510'
Seasons:	May - Oct
Agency:	Sitgreaves NF - Heber RD
Maps:	Woods Canyon, OW Point

"Every tree, every rock, every bush has turned into a soldier" moaned an Indian chief of General Crook's winter campaign of 1871-1872. After the Civil War, the military had little success in protecting settlers from Indian predations. Not until General George C. Crook was appointed Commander of Arizona were they subdued with his innovative strategies. He built roads to move men and supplies into the interior of the wilderness. He hired scouts from peaceful tribes to find and lead troops to warrior strongholds. He always attacked just before dawn for maximum effect and to minimize casualties on both sides. A relic of his efforts is the 150-mile-long Crook Trail which runs by the Rim's edge. Some segments of the original road remain and can be identified by a double slash blazed on the trees. These can be found on the portions that still remain a mile or two south of Willow Springs, and other Rim Lakes.

The sun sparkles off the shimmering waves silhouetting a pair of fisherman drifting lazily across the chilly waters. At Willow Springs Lake you'll find a pleasant, picturesque three-mile walk at the edge of a pine forest on a fisherman's path. Willow Canyon Creek, which runs into Chevelon Canyon, was impounded in 1962 to form this lake. The main access point is the crowded area around the boat ramp. Stroll to the other side of the lake to relax, catch a trout, or speculate on whether the general might have enjoyed the same views.

<u>Directions to Trail Access</u>: **From Payson, at AZ 87 and AZ 260, go east 32 miles on AZ 260 (MP283.5), turn left and go 1 mile north on Willow Springs Lake Rd-FS Rd#149 to the parking area.**

Silhouetted fishermen troll for trout on waters of Willow Springs Lake.

21 - Woods Canyon Lake Trail

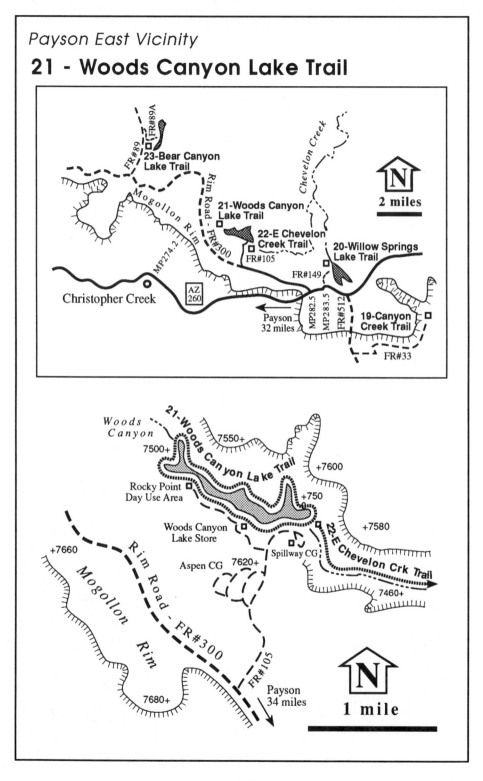

<u>21</u> - Woods Canyon Lake Trail

* Easy walk on dirt and rock path through shady forest around alpine lake.

Rocky Point CG Lake Loop
4.5 mi; 60' gain

Location: Payson - 36 miles E
Elevation: 7500'
Seasons: May - Oct
Agency: Sitgreaves NF-Chevelon RD
Topo map: Woods Canyon

On June 14, 1868, the Navajo nation was released from confinement in New Mexico and began the long walk back to their native land. To renew their lives they were granted necessary provisions, 15,000 sheep, and over three million acres in northeastern Arizona. The sheep herd grew to several hundred thousand by the turn of the century and has been a sustaining force in their lives ever since. Shepherding expanded in the upper plateau region, where one of the area's entrepreneurs, Sam Wood, who worked the Rim, was honored with the namesake Woods Canyon. But the unrestrained shepherding business became too successful because of overgrazing by more than two million sheep. Thus, the Forest Service was forced to adopt a permit system after 1900 to restore the overused environment.

Today there is lush vegetation for the many recreation areas on the Rim. One is Woods Canyon Lake, which is charged by East Chevelon Creek behind a dam constructed in 1956. It is the most popular of the Rim lakes, so you'll find the area crowded in the summer. But you can escape the masses by hiking the scenic, cool, somewhat rocky, five-mile trail that runs along the forest encircling the lake. By the time you get to the other side, all you'll hear is the whoosh of the line from an optimistic fisherman casting for that special trout.

<u>**Directions to Trail Access**</u>: **From Payson, at AZ 87 and AZ 260, go east 32 miles on AZ 260 (MP282.5), turn left on Rim Road-FS Rd#300 and go northwest 3.4 miles to Woods Canyon Lake Road-FS Rd#105. Turn right and go east 1 mile to Rocky Point Picnic Area parking lot.**

Fisherpeople cast for trout from retaining dam at Woods Canyon Lake.

22 - East Chevelon Creek Trail

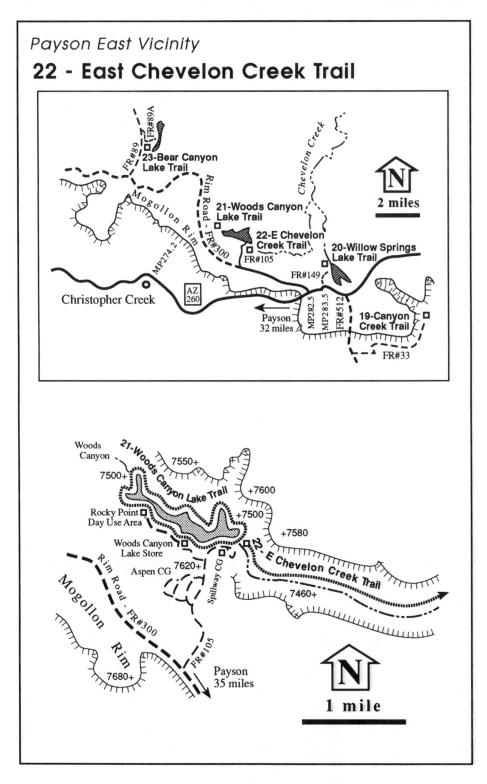

22 - East Chevelon Creek Trail

* Forest walk along grassy creek banks at bottom of shallow canyon.

Spillway CG to Canyon Bend
2.0 mi; 100' loss

Location: Payson - 36 miles E
Elevation: 7460'
Seasons: May - Oct
Agency: Sitgreaves NF-Chevelon RD
Topo map: Woods Canyon

The first pioneers in the territory had to live off the land, but nutritional sources were abundant: large mammals - deer and elk; small game - turkeys, coons, and rabbits; fruits - wild cherries, manzanita berries, and wild squash; and tubers - wild potatoes. However, an early trapper by the name of Chevelon was victimized by a poisonous root growing in the namesake creek that still recalls his misfortune. The 40-mile-long Chevelon Creek, which runs northward into the Little Colorado River, was first settled by Mormons who built 10 cabins half way along the length of the creek. The creek was also homesteaded at its mouth by historian and cattleman Will C. Barnes. However, the settlements had to be abandoned, much to the benefit of the environment, because water flow was undependable in dry years.

You'll discover on this hike the beautiful surroundings that attracted Chevelon and the other pioneers to this area. The unmarked trail starts with a clamber down the dam to the creek. Then follow an unsigned fisherman's path that crisscrosses the creek and extends out along grassy meadows between the forest-lined banks. It is a pretty walk at the cool, high elevation with wildflowers, pine scent, and the soft splashing of the shallow creek.

<u>Directions to Trail Access</u>: **From Payson, at AZ 87 and AZ 260, go east 32 miles on AZ 260 (MP282.5), turn left on Rim Road-FS Rd#300 and go northwest 3.4 miles to Woods Canyon Lake Rd-FS Rd#105. Turn right and go east 1 mile. Bear right and go 0.5 miles to Spillway CG Day Use parking lot. If full, use any area lot and walk east along the shore to access the dam**

It's easy hiking by a lazy stream wandering through a forested meadow.

23 - Bear Canyon Lake Trail

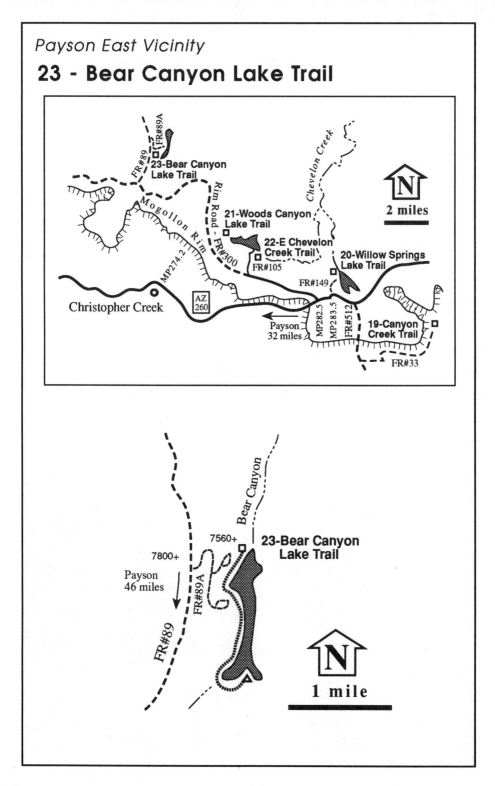

23 - Bear Canyon Lake Trail

* Easy shoreline walk through shady, pine forest by lake in alpine setting.

Parking Lot to Peninsula
2.0 mi; 100' loss

Location:	**Payson - 47 miles E**
Elevation:	**7560'**
Seasons:	**May - Oct**
Agency:	**Sitgreaves NF-Chevelon RD**
Topo map:	**Knoll Lake**

Frontier ranching, hunting, and development has had a devastating effect on native Arizona wildlife. Bear Canyon commemorates the early times, more than a century ago, when hunters told of sometimes seeing a dozen or more grizzlies in a day. But they were eliminated in Arizona by 1935. The state's own native Merriam elk was hunted to extinction and had to be replaced by another species from Colorado. A native red-headed parrot that populated many riparian canyons had disappeared by the turn the century, but efforts are now underway to reintroduce the species from Mexican stock. One of the primitives that still survives is the black bear. They're still here, but are more bashful than grizzlies. You probably won't see one, but it's still a thrill to find a paw print or cairns of bear scat along the trail.

On this hike you'll have a relaxing experience since Bear Canyon Lake, which impounds Willow Springs Creek, is more remote than any of the other more popular Rim lakes. A steep trail runs down from the parking lot and wraps half way around the lake on a flat, easy path at the edge of a pine forest. It extends out onto a little hill on a peninsula that makes a beautiful spot for lunch, napping, or spying on wildlife.

Directions to Trail Access: **From Payson, at AZ 87 and AZ 260, go east 32 miles on AZ 260 (MP282.5), turn left on Rim Road (FS Rd#300) and go northwest 12 mi to FS Rd#89. Go east 2 miles to Bear Canyon Lake Road (FS Rd#89A). Turn right and go south 0.5 miles. Turn left and go 0.1 mile to the lot. Walk down to the shore and take the trail to the peninsula.**

Hikers pause to study wildflowers on bank of Bear Canyon Lake.

Area V. Payson West Trails

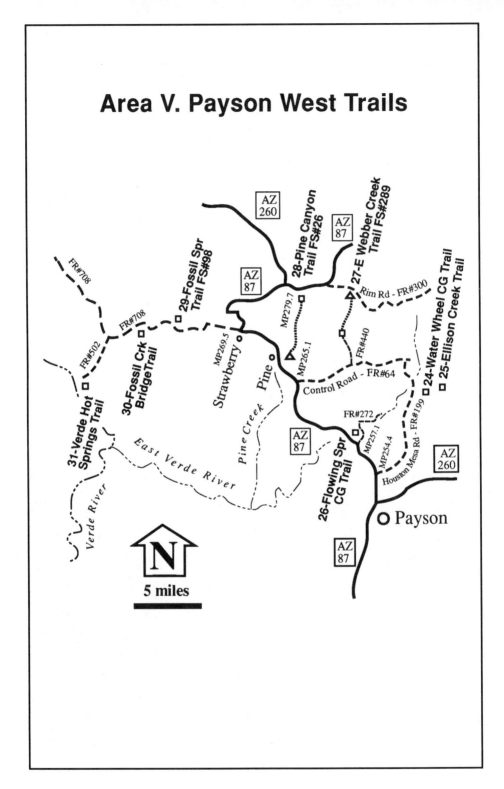

FR#708

AZ 260

28-Pine Canyon Trail FS#26

AZ 87

27-E Webber Creek Trail FS#289

29-Fossil Spr Trail FS#98

AZ 87

Rim Rd - FR#300

24-Water Wheel CG Trail

25-Ellison Creek Trail

FR#708

MP279.7

FR#502

MP269.5

Strawberry

MP265.1

FR#440

30-Fossil Crk Bridge Trail

Pine

Control Road - FR#64

Pine Creek

FR#272

FR#199

AZ 260

31-Verde Hot Springs Trail

MP257.1

Houston Mesa Rd - FR#199

MP254.4

East Verde River

AZ 87

26-Flowing Spr CG Trail

Verde River

N

5 miles

O Payson

AZ 87

Area V.
Payson West Vicinity

HIKE DESCRIPTIONS & LOCAL MAPS

24 - East Verde River - Water Wheel Campground Trail

25 - Ellison Creek Trail

26 - East Verde River - Flowing Springs Campground Trail

27 - East Webber Creek Trail FS#289

28 - Pine Canyon Trail FS#26

29 - Fossil Springs Trail FS#98

30 - Fossil Creek - Bridge Trail

31 - Verde River - Verde Hot Springs Trail

Hikers scramble by conflunece of Ellison Creek and East Verde River.

24 - Water Wheel CG Trail

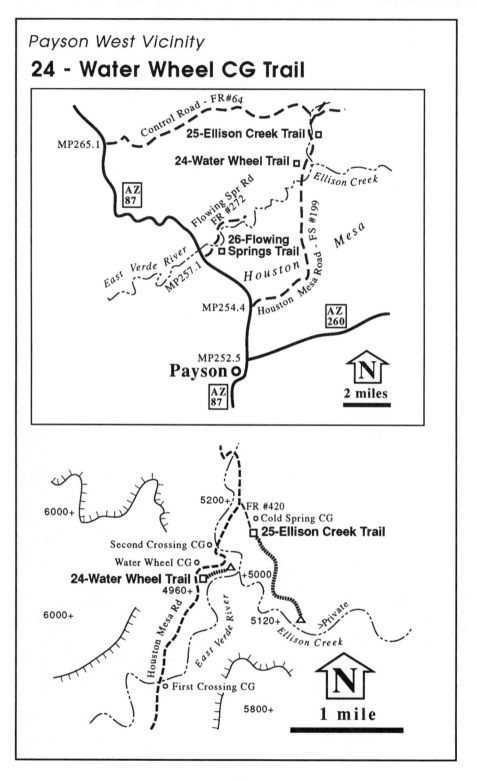

<u>24</u> - East Verde River - Water Wheel CG Trail

* Short hike along sandy bank of East Verde to swim hole and waterfall.

Water Wheel CG to Waterfall
0.3 mi; 40' gain

Location: Payson - 10 mi N
Elevation: 4960'
Seasons: Apr - Oct
Agency: Tonto NF - Payson RD
Topo map: Payson North

"Shoot, you damn idiots! What do you suppose I gave you ammunition for -- to eat?" Such was the colorful language that Major Adna Romanza Chaffee used to spur his troops on in battle. Chaffee commanded at the Battle of Big Dry Wash on July 6, 1872, which was the last major conflict of the Indian campaigns in Arizona. A band of renegade warriors from Cibique had planned an ambush of the troops at a ridge on the Mogollon Rim. But scout Al Sieber suspected this and warned Chaffee, so he was able to circle his troops and ambush the warriors instead. The battle began in late afternoon and lasted until a fearsome storm struck at nightfall, depositing four inches of hail. At the end of the battle, 16 warriors had died, three Medals of Honor were recommended, and major Indian hostilities in Arizona had ceased.

On the short hike from Water Wheel Campground, you'll find the scenery of the rocky pine forest similar to that of the battleground which lies a dozen miles to the northeast. The stroll on the sandy bank of the East Verde leads east a quarter mile to a craggy, double-tiered, 40' high waterfall. It plummets into a refreshing swimming hole with fine, clear water. If you go east another quarter mile and climb the rocky hill, you'll see where Ellison Creek cascades into the East Verde. This area, and the length of the river, was once a thoroughfare for itinerant Indian bands, but only before the white man arrived more than a century ago.

<u>**Directions to Campground**</u>: **From Payson, at AZ 87 and AZ 260, go northwest two miles on AZ 87 (MP254.4), turn right on to Houston Mesa Road (FS Rd#199), go 7.9 miles north, park by Water Wheel Campground.**

East Verde River cascades down the forty-foot high water wheel.

91

25 - Ellison Creek Trail

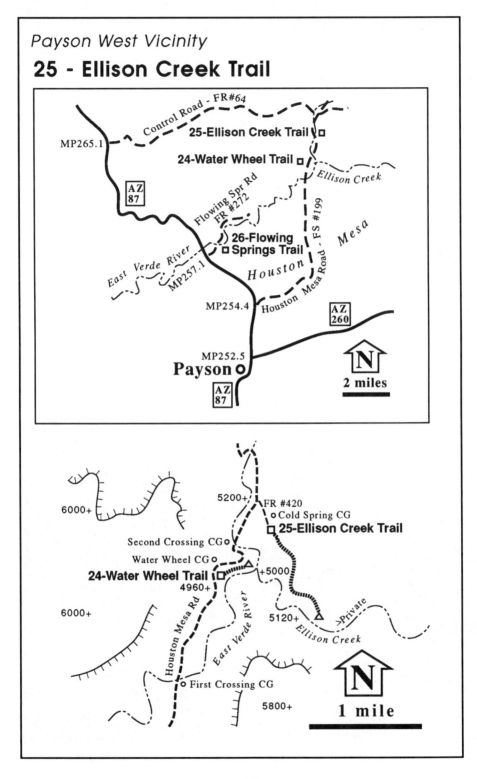

<u>25</u> - Ellison Creek Trail

* Hike down old jeep road and over shallow basalt slabs to waterfall.

FS Rd#420 Camp Area to Waterfall **1.5 mi; 160' loss + 60' gain**	**Location:** Payson - 10 mi N **Elevation:** 5200' **Seasons:** Apr - Oct **Agency:** Tonto NF - Payson RD **Topo map:** Payson North

In the late 1800s, Arizona Territory was a land of opportunity with its mineral wealth and open range. Colonel Jesse W. Ellison, rancher and veteran of the Civil War, seized the opportunity. In 1885, he left Texas with 3000 head of cattle that were transported by rail to Bowie Station near the eastern edge of Arizona. He and his cowhands drove the herd to the area north of Payson by the creek that now bears his name. In 1894, he moved to the meadows of Pleasant Valley and established Q Ranch. He and his ranch hands homesteaded land until they accumulated over 2000 acres. He had a daughter who married W.P. Hunt, who became the state's first governor. Ellison died in 1915 at the age of 71 and is buried with his wife, daughter, and the governor in Hunt's Pyramid at the top of Papago Park in Phoenix.

You can experience a bit of the spectacular scenery that the colonel enjoyed along Ellison Creek. It is a moderately easy hike from the camping area down an old jeep trail a mile to the creek. From there, it is another half mile of climbing some shallow basalt slabs to reach the forty-foot cascading waterfall and pools. Beyond the waterfall is private property which is not accessible. The pools make a nice place for a picnic and some wading. And we didn't have to share our seat on the ledges with any thirsty cows or inquisitive bulls.

<u>**Directions to Trail Access**</u>: **From Payson, at AZ 87 and AZ 260, go northwest 2 miles on AZ 87 (MP254.4), turn right on to Houston Mesa Road (FS Rd#199) and go 8.1 miles N to the unmarked FS Rd#420. Turn right and go 0.2 miles to the camping area. Park and hike down jeep road.**

Ellison Creek cascades down tiered waterfall into pools at base of cliff.

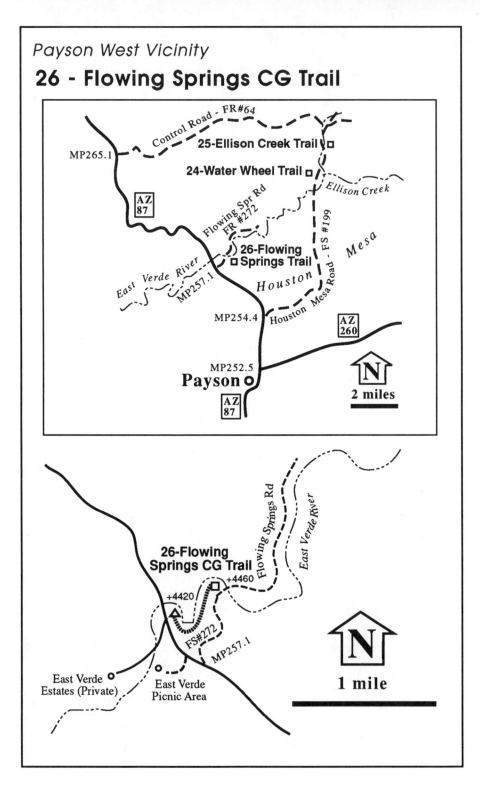

Payson West Vicinity

26 - Flowing Springs CG Trail

Control Road - FR#64

25-Ellison Creek Trail

MP265.1

24-Water Wheel Trail

Ellison Creek

AZ 87

Flowing Spr Rd FR #272

26-Flowing Springs Trail

Houston Mesa Road - FS #199

Mesa

Houston

East Verde River

MP257.1

MP254.4

Houston Mesa Road

AZ 260

MP252.5

Payson

AZ 87

N

2 miles

Flowing Springs Rd

East Verde River

26-Flowing Springs CG Trail

+4460

+4420

FS#272

MP257.1

East Verde Estates (Private)

East Verde Picnic Area

N

1 mile

<u>26</u> - East Verde River - Flowing Springs Trail

* Hike along rocky creek bank into lichen covered red rock canyon.

Flowing Springs CG to pools
    0.8 mi; 40' loss

Location: Payson - 8 mi N
Elevation: 4460'
Seasons: Apr - Oct
Agency: Tonto NF - Payson RD
Topo map: Payson North

    King S. Woolsey was a frontier entrepreneur who was regarded as the leading citizen of Arizona Territory in the 1870s. He was born in Alabama, raised in Louisiana, filibustered in Cuba, mined in California, and then packed in Yuma in 1860, all by the age of 28. He planned on fighting for the Confederacy, but while en route to join, he instead purchased Agua Caliente Ranch and ended up providing supplies for Union troops. On the Walker gold expedition in 1863, he founded Agua Fria Ranch near Prescott in partnership with Governor Goodwin. While there, he led expeditions against Indian bands and discovered the East Verde River along the way. After having financial problems, he migrated south, became a major land owner, and organized Phoenix Flour Mills. He was also elected representative to the Territorial Legislature five times. But he died early, at the age 47, of apoplexy and his memory has been honored by the place names of Woolsey Peak and Woolsey Creek.

    One pleasant access point along the 56 mile length of the East Verde River is at Flowing Springs Campground. The river flows year round because water is pumped from the Rim by a copper mining company which has an exchange agreement with the state. Park or camp at the campground and walk over to the river for an easy day hike. You can go a mile west to a deep canyon with lichen covered red rock formations or you can go wander eastward up to two miles past some beautiful meadows and three other campgrounds.

    <u>Directions to Trail Access</u>: **Starting in Payson, at AZ 87 and AZ 260, go northwest 4.6 miles on AZ 87 (MP257.1), turn right on to Flowing Springs Road (FS Rd#622) and go 3 miles east, park by campground lot.**

Six inch trout relax in shallow pools along East Verde River.

27 - East Webber Creek Trail FS#289

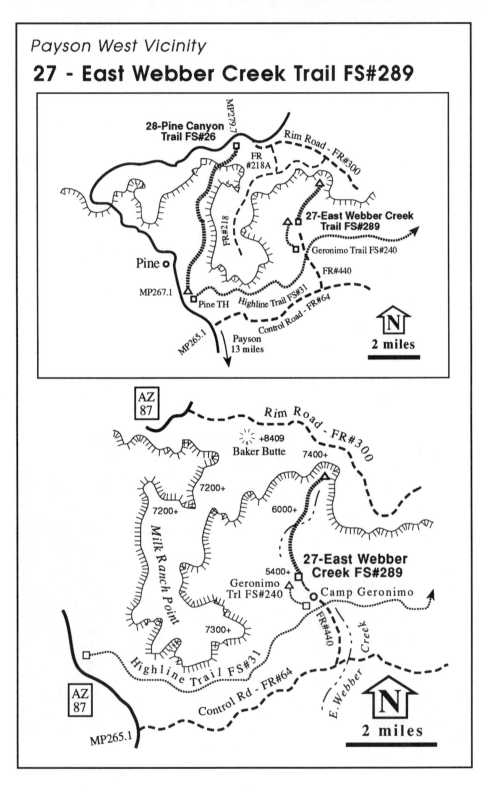

27 - East Webber Creek Trail FS#289

* Hike by creek with columbine and moss-covered boulders.

Geronimo Camp to Trailhead
   0.5 mi; 60' gain
Geronimo Camp to Boulders
   3.8 mi; 960' gain

Location: Payson - 20 mi N
Elevation: 5400'
Seasons: Apr - Oct
Agency: Tonto NF - Payson Dist.
Topo map: Kehl Ridge

     The boom-bust times of frontier mining towns attracted characters that made law and order a dangerous task for local sheriffs. One of the most famous was John Henry Thompson, a tall, affable Texan who arrived in Arizona in 1880 at age 19. He homesteaded on Webber Creek and was called Rimrock Henry. A few years later, an unexpected vacancy opened up for sheriff in the boom town of Globe. Thompson ran for the position, won it, and served a record seven terms. In that time he tracked down and brought to justice more than a half dozen killers. He also saved the lives of three prisoners from angry lynch mobs. After his dedicated service, he returned to ranching and mining interests near Globe.

     The trail along the upper quarter of the 15-mile-long East Webber Creek is a streamside route through an enchanting forest of pine, oak, ash, and walnut. The trail winds upward at a moderate slope back and forth across the creek in a forest decorated with butterflies, birds, lichen, and moss. Supposedly, the route runs up to the top of the Rim, but we stopped for lunch at a scenic spot by a large rockfall above a trickling spring. It is clear that Thompson was as lucky a homesteader as he was a sheriff.

     <u>**Directions to Trailhead**</u>: **From Payson, at AZ 87 and AZ 260, go northwest 12.6 miles on AZ 87 (MP265.1), turn right on the Control Road (FS Rd#64) and go 6 miles east, go north 2 miles on FS Rd#440 to Geronimo Scout Camp and park nearby. Access the trailhead through Geronimo Scout Camp (with permission) or go around the camp on the Geronimo Trail.**

Sycamore, pine, ash, and walnut all shade East Webber Trail along creek.

28 - Pine Canyon Trail FS#26

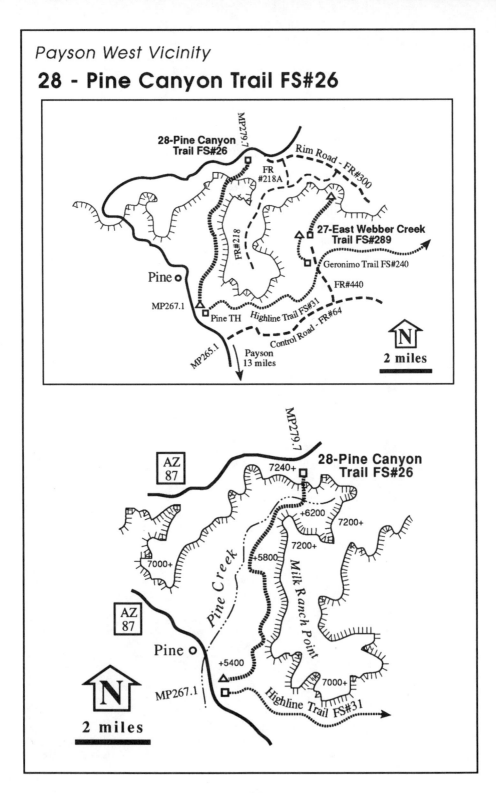

28-Pine Canyon
Trail FS#26

MP279.7

Rim Road - FR#300

FR
#218A

FR#218

27-East Webber Creek
Trail FS#289

Geronimo Trail FS#240

FR#440

Pine o

MP267.1

Pine TH

Highline Trail FS#31

Control Road - FR#64

MP265.1

Payson
13 miles

N

2 miles

MP279.7

AZ
87

7240+

28-Pine Canyon
Trail FS#26

+6200

7200+

7200+

7000+

+5800

Pine Creek

Milk Ranch Point

AZ
87

Pine o

+5400

MP267.1

7000+

Highline Trail FS#31

N

2 miles

28 - Pine Canyon Trail FS#26

* Hike along cool, mossy creek in Ponderosa pine forest.

North TH to Rim Base   **Location:** Payson - 27 mi N
    4.0 mi; 1440' loss   **Elevation:** 7240'
North TH to Pine TH   **Seasons:** Apr - Oct
    8.0 mi; 1400' loss + 400' gain   **Agency:** Tonto NF - Payson RD
                                      Topo map: Pine

The logging industry in Arizona began more than a century ago and still employs some 2,500 workers today. Many work along the Mogollon Rim, the location of the world's largest Ponderosa pine forest. The first buildings in the Payson area were constructed from logs, but boards and planks had greater utility, so the first sawmill was constructed. It stood on the site of the present Kaibab mill. Two more sawmills were built in Pine. The first one was located on Pine Creek just below the Rim and was driven by water plunging from a large spring. However, the spring's flow slowed and the mill had to be moved. Logging on the Rim continues today, but with mixed benefits. Only when the area's resources are replenished at the rate at which they are consumed will the environment's future stability be assured.

Pine Creek Trail may be accessed from the upper or lower trailhead. Starting from the top of the Rim, the trail runs down a mile through the pines past the site of the old sawmill. It then runs two miles along the creek that has mossy rocks, fern covered banks, and butterflies flitting across the water. This is the best part of the trail, so I'd advise turning around here and going back to the Rim. You can also continue south four miles on the warm, strenuous route to the lower trailhead. Another option is to start at that trailhead just south of Pine. From here the trail goes a hot two miles up a 400' rise, down two miles in the forest, then up two miles and 1400' along the creek, and finally a mile across the Rim to the upper trailhead.

Directions to Trailhead: From Payson, at AZ 87 and AZ 260, go northwest 27 miles on AZ 87 and park at the trailhead turnoff (MP279.7).

Delicate columbine light up the banks of the Pine Creek Trail.

29 - Fossil Springs Trail FS#98

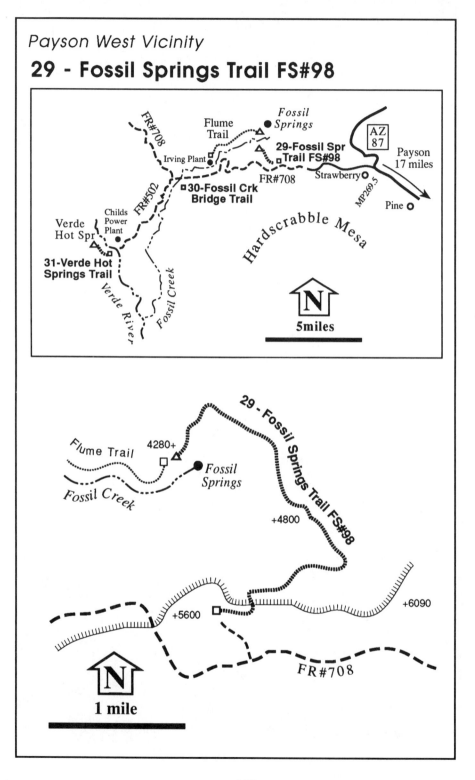

<u>29</u> - Fossil Springs Trail FS#98

* Hike down winding old jeep road to lush, riparian springs.

Trailhead to Fossil Springs
     2.5 mi; 1320' loss

Special: Fossil Springs Wilderness

Location: Payson - 22 mi NW
Elevation: 5600'
Seasons: Apr - Oct
Agency: Tonto NF - Payson RD
Topo map: Strawberry

     Today, wilderness areas offer adventurers the same sense of discovery that the unspoiled land offered settlers a century ago. King Woolsey discovered and named Fossil Creek and Springs while tracking Indians in 1864. The million gallons of 72F water that gush from the springs every hour have created a lush environment which supports over 30 types of trees and bushes and over 100 species of birds. The walls near the springs contain small fossils from an ancient sea that washed over the area 350 million years ago. Unfortunately, just to the south, a flume was built in 1916 to supply water to the Irving and Childs Power Plants which first supplied Phoenix with electricity. Any further intrusions are now prohibited since the area became the 12,000-acre Fossil Springs Wilderness in 1984.

     The upper trail to the springs follows a steep, dusty, hot old jeep road two miles down past an old gravel pit. The trail turns south and goes a half mile to Fossil Springs. There is an alternative route, the Flume Trail, that can be accessed five miles further along the road. From the parking area by Childs Power Plant, an old jeep road follows the moderately sloped flume to the springs. From either trail you can discover the little Shangri La where you can swim, picnic, study fossils, or explore the aqua waters of travertine pools along the creek.

     <u>**Directions to Trailhead**</u>: **From Payson, at AZ 87 and AZ 260, go northwest 17 miles on AZ 87 (MP269.5), turn left on FS Rd#708 (at Strawberry Inn) and go 4 miles southwest to a dirt road, turn right and go north 0.5 miles to the trailhead lot.**

Verdant growth is nurtured by a million gallons-per-hour at Fossil Springs.

30 - Fossil Creek Bridge Trail

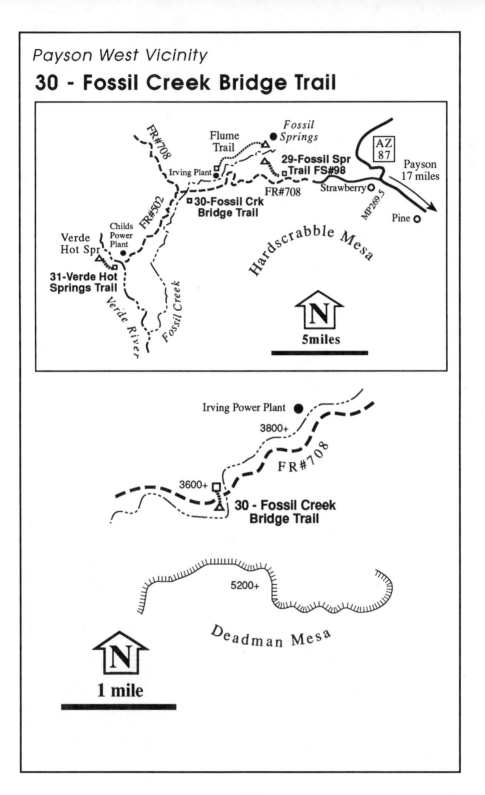

<u>30</u> - Fossil Creek Bridge Trail

* Short scramble down to creek and pool lined with travertine deposits.

Fossil Creek Bridge to Pool
0.2 mi; 80' loss

Special: Mazatzal Wilderness

Location: Payson - 28 mi NW
Elevation: 3600'
Seasons: Apr - Oct
Agency: Tonto NF - Payson RD
Topo map: Strawberry

Place names are curious things, sometimes commemorating historic events and sometimes prosaic incidents. Military encounters were often recognized, as with Battleground Ridge, which recalls the Battle of Big Dry Wash on the Mogollon Rim in 1882. A canyon called Dorens Defeat, located a couple of miles west of the Fossil Creek Bridge, seemed like it might remember an incident where some fresh, young lieutenant's patrol might have been ambushed by a band of hostile Indians. But you won't find any such encounter listed in the Military Record. Instead, the place name simply refers to a trusty old mule named Doren, once owned by pioneer C.C. Calloway, who "met his Waterloo" in his namesake canyon.

Just down from the Fossil Creek Bridge is a beautiful swimming hole with turquoise waters that make it look like a little bit of Havasupai. The waters of Fossil Creek spring from ground rich in lime, which is then laid down along the length of the creek as travertine deposits. To enjoy the swimming hole and the scenery along the creek, you can park your car just past the bridge and scramble down the steep slope. It is an ideal spot for a dip, a picnic lunch, or a short hike further down the luxuriously-colored waterway.

Directions to Trail Access: **From Payson, at AZ 87 and AZ 260, go northwest 17 miles on AZ 87 (MP269.5), turn left on FS Rd#708 (at Strawberry Inn) and and go 11 miles southwest to the bridge over Fossil Creek. Pull off just past bridge. Note: this road is a narrow, steep, winding route not suitable for travel in poor weather or with acrophobics.**

Fossil Creek turns azure blue from travertine deposits lining pool.

31 - Verde Hot Springs Trail

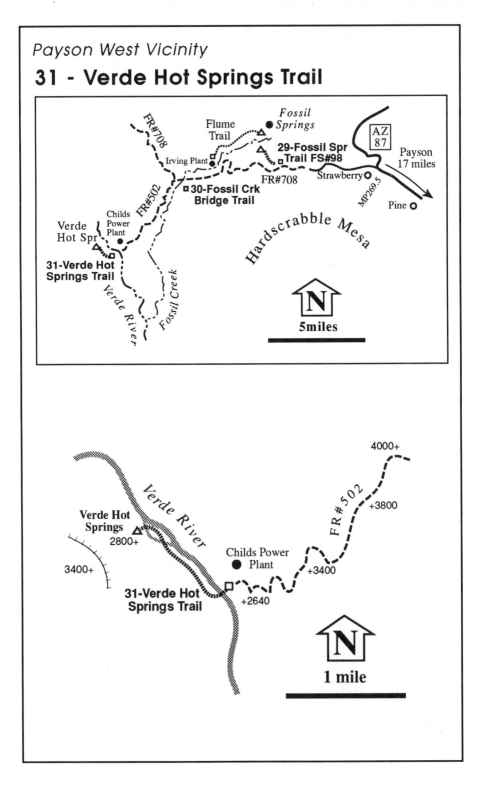

<u>31</u> - Verde River - Verde Hot Springs Trail

* Hike along the Verde River to old resort ruins and hot spring.

Childs Plant CG to Hot Springs
       0.7 mi; 160' gain

Location: Payson - 35 mi NW
Elevation: 2640'
Seasons: May - Nov
Agency: Tonto NF - Payson RD
Topo map: Verde Hot Springs

The pungent, soothing waters of hot springs dot the southwestern landscape and were thought by Indians and settlers alike to have curative powers. The twentieth century moderns evidently agreed, because they built a modern resort at Verde Hot Springs. The retreat sat safely thirty feet above the sometimes tempestuous Verde River on a long, wide ledge extending out from a creek bank wall. Visitors enjoyed fine views that extended miles up and down the verdant valley along the river. Unfortunately, the grounds were swept by fire in the 1950s and the land lease was terminated by the Forest Service. All that remains of the lush resort are the hotel foundation, a small rock house, and a concrete 8' x 10' hot spring pool.

The hike starts from Childs Power Plant campground by wading across the Verde River. (Call the Forest Service before visiting - high water can be dangerous.) Then follow an old jeep trail west for a half mile and cross over to an island in the middle of the river. Go another quarter mile and look up on the river's south bank where you'll see the old stone house that sits next to the hot springs. Wade across deeper water here. Or go another quarter mile to cross in shallow water and follow the old road back to the hot springs. Try out the 95F waters and judge whether they are not only relaxing, but also regenerative.

<u>Directions to Trail Access</u>: **From Payson, at AZ 87 and AZ 260, go northwest 17 miles on AZ 87 (MP269.5), turn left on FS Rd#708 (at Strawberry Inn) and go 11.8 miles southwest. Turn left on FS Rd#502 and go south 5.8 miles to CG lot (last 0.2 miles requires a high clearance vehicle).**

High ground of Verde Hot Spring affords fine view of Verde River habitat.

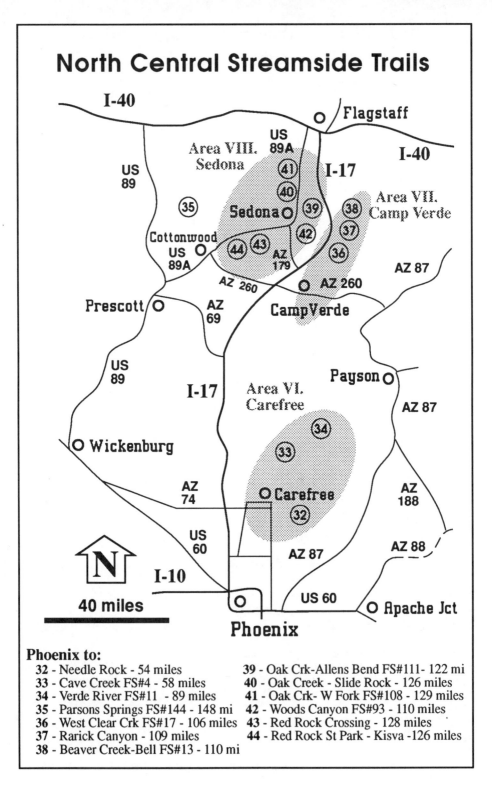

North Central Streamside Trails

I-40

Flagstaff

I-40

US 89A

Area VIII. Sedona

I-17

US 89

㊶

㊵

㉟

Sedona

㊴

㊳

Area VII. Camp Verde

Cottonwood

US 89A

㊸ ㊸

AZ 179

㊷

㊳

㊲

㊱

AZ 87

AZ 260

AZ 260

Prescott

AZ 69

CampVerde

US 89

I-17

Area VI. Carefree

Payson

AZ 87

O Wickenburg

㉞

㉝

AZ 74

Carefree

US 60

㉜

AZ 188

AZ 87

AZ 88

US 60

N

40 miles

I-10

Phoenix

US 60

Apache Jct

Phoenix to:

32 - Needle Rock - 54 miles
33 - Cave Creek FS#4 - 58 miles
34 - Verde River FS#11 - 89 miles
35 - Parsons Springs FS#144 - 148 mi
36 - West Clear Crk FS#17 - 106 miles
37 - Rarick Canyon - 109 miles
38 - Beaver Creek-Bell FS#13 - 110 mi

39 - Oak Crk-Allens Bend FS#111- 122 mi
40 - Oak Creek - Slide Rock - 126 miles
41 - Oak Crk- W Fork FS#108 - 129 miles
42 - Woods Canyon FS#93 - 110 miles
43 - Red Rock Crossing - 128 miles
44 - Red Rock St Park - Kisva -126 miles

Ch. 6 North Central Arizona Trails

Area VI. Carefree Vicinity

32 - Verde River - Needle Rock Trail

33 - Cave Creek Trail FS#4

34 - Verde River - Sheep Bridge - Trail FS#11

Area VII. Camp Verde Vicinity

35 - Sycamore Creek - Parson Springs Trail FS#144

36 - West Clear Creek Trail FS#17

37 - Rarick Canyon Trail

38 - Wet Beaver Creek - Bell Trail FS#13

Area VIII. Sedona Vicinity

39 - Oak Creek - Allens Bend Trail FS#111

40 - Oak Creek - Slide Rock State Park - Creek Trail

41 - West Fork Oak Creek Trail FS#108

42 - Dry Beaver Creek - Woods Canyon Trail FS#93

43 - Oak Creek - Red Rock Crossing Trail

44 - Oak Creek - Red Rock State Park - Kisva Trail

View at Needle Rock of Verde River emerging from Mazatzal Mountains.

Area VI. Carefree Trails

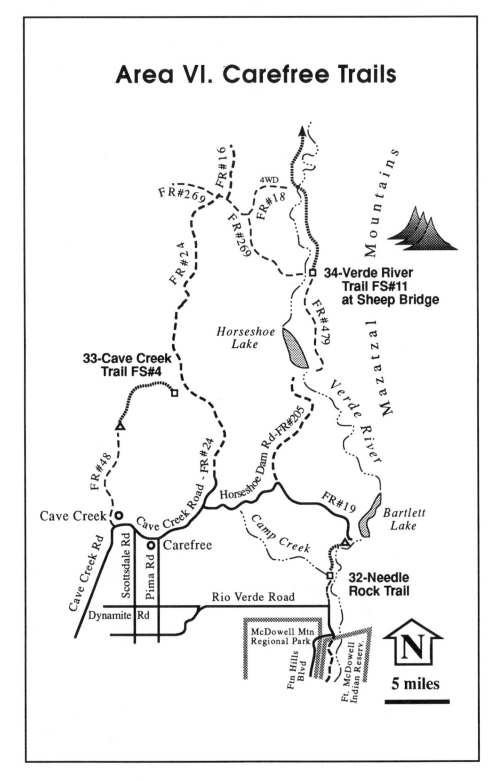

FR#16

FR#269

4WD

FR#18

FR#24

FR#269

Mountains

34-Verde River
Trail FS#11
at Sheep Bridge

Horseshoe
Lake

FR#479

33-Cave Creek
Trail FS#4

Mazatzal

Verde River

Horseshoe Dam Rd-FR#205

Cave Creek Road - FR#24

FR#48

Cave Creek

Scottsdale Rd

Pima Rd

Carefree

Camp Creek

FR#19

Bartlett
Lake

32-Needle
Rock Trail

Cave Creek Rd

Rio Verde Road

Dynamite Rd

McDowell Mtn
Regional Park

Ftn Hills Blvd

Ft. McDowell
Indian Reserv.

N

5 miles

Area VI.
Carefree Vicinity

HIKE DESCRIPTIONS & LOCAL MAPS

32 - Verde River - Needle Rock Trail

33 - Cave Creek Trail FS#4

34 - Verde River at Sheep Bridge - Verde River Trail FS#11

Hikers wind down path toward swimming hole on Cave Creek Trail.

32 - Needle Rock Trail

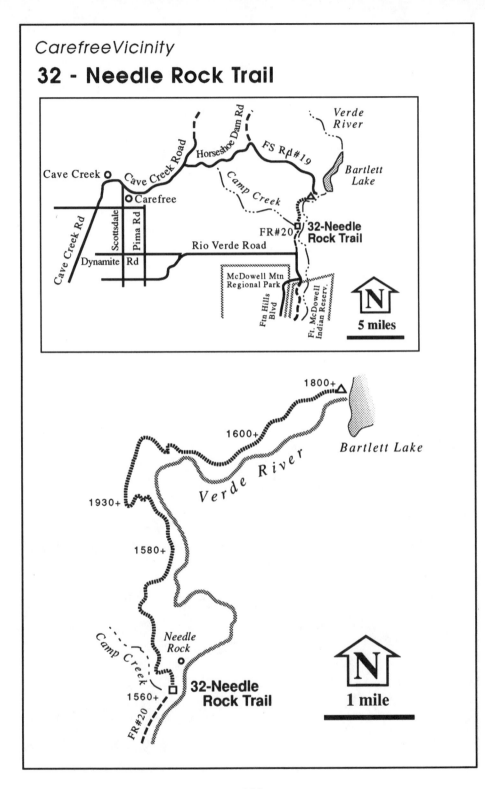

<u>32</u> - Verde River - Needle Rock Trail

* A hilly walk near flood plain and riparian environment of Verde River.

Needle Rock Park to Hill Vista	**Location:**	Carefree - 28 mi SE
1.5 mi; 160' gain	**Elevation:**	1560'
Needle Rock Park to Horseshoe Dam	**Seasons:**	Sep - Nov
5.0 mi; 500' gain	**Agency:**	Tonto NF - Cave Creek RD
Special: Wildlife - Closed 12/1-6/30	**Topo map:**	Bartlett Dam

By 1885, more than 100 frontier Army camps and forts had been established for protecting settlers. Ironically, many of the forts were later transformed into tribal reservations. In 1872, Ft. McDowell was incorporated to control southeastern Yavapai and Tonto Apache tribes in the Salt and Tonto River Basins. In 1873, there were 1500 Yavapai who surrendered to General Crook at Camp Verde. Two years later the government ordered them on a 200-mile winter march to the San Carlos Reservation which resulted in 240 deaths. It wasn't until 1903 that a group of 200 of the remaining Yavapai were finally permitted to establish their own reservation at Ft. McDowell. Since then, the tribe has grown to 700 members.

The Needle Rock Trail lies north of the reservation and runs on an old jeep trail along the west bank of the Verde River to Bartlett Dam. It is a primitive, unmarked route which starts from the parking lot and rises northward on a hill to fine vistas, including the reservation to the south. It then moves up and down a series of hilly old jeep trails and then finally down to the river bank. Generally bear right, toward the river, to stay on the trail. You can stop after a mile and a half at athe river or head up a rise on the full route to Horseshoe Dam.

<u>**Directions to Trail Access**</u>: **From Carefree, at Scottsdale Road and Cave Creek Road, go south 7 miles. Turn left and go 15 miles on Dynamite Blvd and Rio Verde Road. Turn left on FS Rd#20 and go N 6 miles to the parking area. (From Fountain Hills, at Shea Blvd, go north 13 miles on Fountain Hills Blvd, jog east and go N 6 miles on FS Rd#20 to the lot.)**

Panoramic view of Verde River desert floodplain from hill top along trail.

33 - Cave Creek Trail FS#4

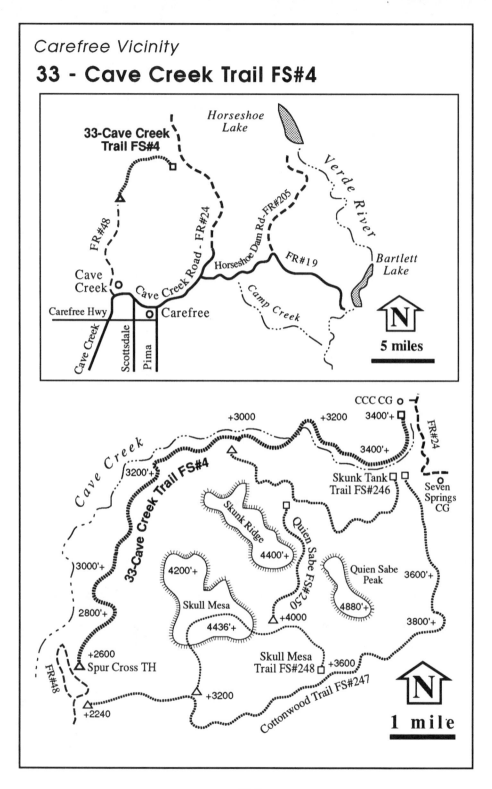

33-Cave Creek
Trail FS#4

Horseshoe Lake

Verde River

FR#48

Horseshoe Dam Rd.- FR#205

Cave Creek Road - FR#24

Cave Creek

Horseshoe Dam Rd.

FR#19

Bartlett Lake

Carefree Hwy

Carefree

Camp Creek

Cave Creek

Scottsdale

Pima

N

5 miles

CCC CG

+3000   +3200   3400'+   FR#24

3400'+

Cave Creek

3200'+

Skunk Tank
Trail FS#246

Seven
Springs
CG

33-Cave Creek Trail FS#4

Skunk Ridge

4400'+

Quien Sabe FS#250

Quien Sabe
Peak

3600'+

3000'+

4200'+

4880'+

2800'+

Skull Mesa

4436'+

+4000

3800'+

+2600

Spur Cross TH

Skull Mesa
Trail FS#248   +3600

FR#48

+3200

+2240

Cottonwood Trail FS#247

N

1 mile

112

33 - Cave Creek Trail FS#4

* Up and down hills of chaparral-covered canyon by picturesque creek.

Cave Creek TH to Swim Hole	Location:	Carefree - 18 mi NE
2.5 mi; 400' loss	Elevation:	3400'
Cave Creek TH to Spur Cross TH	Seasons:	Oct - Apr
9.7 mi; 1200' gain	Agency:	Tonto NF - Cave Creek RD
	Maps:	New River Mesa, Humboldt Mtn

Some of Arizona's early miners achieved a small measure of wealth from their claims, while others staked a lasting claim in Arizona history with their place names. Ed Caves, a miner working the hills north of Phoenix in the 1880s, was occasionally mentioned in the local news. He was nicknamed old Rackensack, for a mine he discovered four miles north of Camp Creek. Although the mine has long since been out of production, Caves memory endures as the place name for today's well recognized town and 20-mile-long creek.

The trail begins unassumingly by first moving over a small rise and then down next to and along a dry portion of the bed of Cave Creek. In a mile or so, the creek comes to life as the trail heads upward and then undulates up and down along the creek's shallow canyon walls. Hiking is finest in the spring when the hills effervesce with a spectacular display of wildflowers like the creamy orange Mexican poppies dotting small fields of lavender lupine. Hiking in the spring or fall is very warm, but tolerable. In the summer, the trail is blazing hot, and the only reason for venturing out would be the swimming holes at three and five miles. In the winter the mornings are frigid, but thaw into warm afternoons that make for pleasant hiking when the trails on the Mogollon Rim remain snow covered and frozen solid.

Directions to Trailhead: From Carefree, at Scottsdale and Cave Creek Roads, go east 6 miles on Cave Creek Road into FS Rd#24. Continue northeast on FS Rd#24 another 12 miles just past (50 yards) the CCC CG. Pull into the lot on the west side of the road for the creek and trailhead.

Hikers relax near shallow pool on the Cave Creek Trail.

113

34 - Verde River Trail FS#11

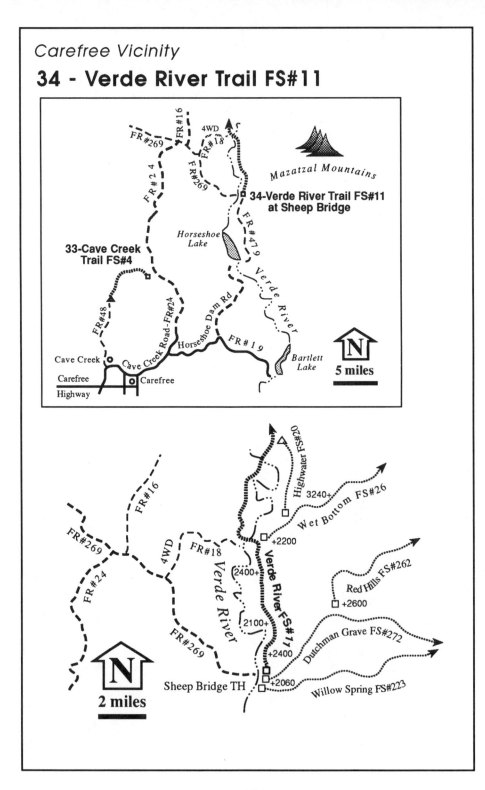

<u>34</u> - Verde River at Sheep Bridge Trail FS#11

* Cross Verde on Sheep Bridge and walk along open riparian habitat.

FS Rd#269 TH across Bridge	Location: Carefree - 49 mi NE
1.0 mi; 340' gain	Elevation: 2060'
FS Rd#269 TH to North Crossing	Seasons: Nov - Mar
8.0 mi; 580' gain	Agency: Tonto NF-Cave Creek RD
Special: Mazatzal Wilderness	Topo map: Wet Bottom Mesa, Chalk Mtn

Arizona shepherding began in 1540 when Coronado brought 5000 sheep on his trip to locate the fabled Seven Cities of Cibola. Over the next two centuries, the Navajos developed herds on the Upper Plateau in northern Arizona. By the late 1890s, settlers' herds grew beyond a million sheep in the same area The profession expanded southwest to the Verde River with the first grazing permit in 1910. When numbers exceeded 11,000, Sheep Bridge was constructed in 1941 to allow for travel between summer and winter ranges. But in the 1950s synthetic fibers led to the decline of the sheep industry. When the last herd crossed the bridge in 1979, it fell into disrepair and was destroyed in 1988. However, hunters, hikers, and ranchers lobbied for a replacement and in 1990 a new steel bridge was dedicated.

A visit to the bridge is a rough, but scenic driving experience. Once there you can camp, enjoy the sandy beaches, or take advantage of opportunities for wilderness hiking into the Mazatzals and for scenic hikes along the Verde. One pleasant and panoramic route runs northward up and down a hilly route on Verde River Trail FS#11, for up to eight miles, to a water crossing where you can set up a car shuttle when you cross back over the river.

<u>Directions to Trailhead</u>: From Carefree, at Scottsdale Road and Cave Creek Road, go northeast 37 miles on Cave Creek Road (at 6 miles it turns into FS Rd#24). Turn right on to FS Rd#269 and go southeast 12 miles to Sheep Bridge and the trailhead.

Scenic Mazatzals can be accessed across Sheep Bridge.

115

Area VII. Camp Verde Trails

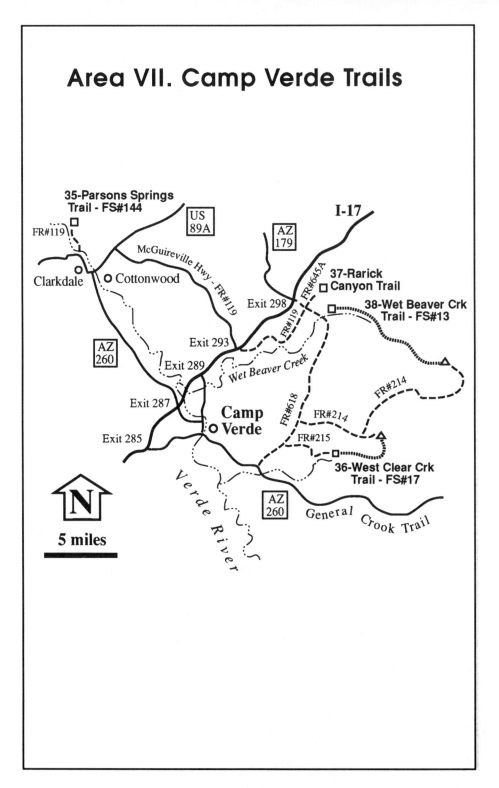

116

Area VII.
Camp Verde Vicinity

HIKE DESCRIPTIONS & LOCAL MAPS

35 - Sycamore Creek - Parsons Spring Trail FS#144

36 - West Clear Creek Trail FS#17

37 - Rarick Canyon Creek Trail

38 - Wet Beaver Creek - Bell Trail FS#13

Hikers head into Sycamore Canyon on Parsons Spring Trail.

35 - Parson's Springs Trail FS#144

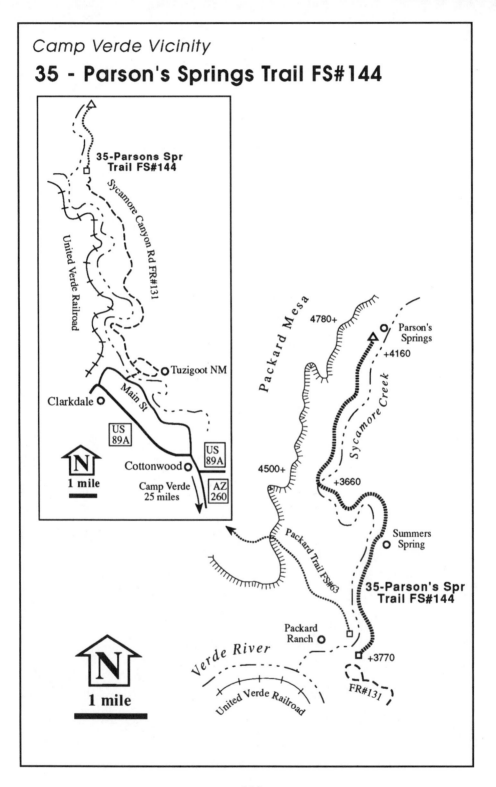

<u>35</u> - Sycamore Creek - Parson's Springs Trail FS#144

* Moderately easy walk along red rock canyon with fine swimming holes.

Parking Lot to Swim Hole	**Location:**	**Camp Verde - 45 miles NW**
1.5 mi; 200' loss	**Elevation:**	**3600'**
Parking Lot to Parson's Springs	**Seasons:**	**Mar - Nov**
3.5 mi; 200'loss + 500'gain	**Agency:**	**Prescott NF - Prescott RD**
Special: Sycamore Wilderness	**Maps:**	**ClarkdaleSE, Sycamore Basin**

Thoughts of gold or silver may have quickened the pulse of prospectors in Arizona in the 1860s and 70s, but by 1888, and thereafter, copper was the sustaining metal of the mining industry in the state. Production of the ruddy metal exceeded $100 million per year many times in the early 1900s. With improved transportation, ore was moved from rugged mountains to flatland smelters. In 1911, a railroad line was completed that ran along the Verde River from the United Verde mine in Jerome to a new smelter in Clarkdale. Look south of the trailhead and you'll see that line which, instead of ore, now carries tourists along a river decorated with colorful wildflowers, red rock grottoes, and soaring bald eagles.

The hike up Sycamore Canyon to Parson's Springs is pretty as a picture too. The first half mile is exposed and descends a few hundred feet into a red rock canyon that frames the creek. It's a cool walk through an oak, cottonwood and sycamore forest. At a mile, you'll see watercress surrounding fresh springs that feed the creek. Another half mile takes you to a sunny swimming hole. And after another two more miles and a few creek crossings, you'll find a swampy area that is Parson's Springs.

<u>**Directions to Trailhead**</u>: From Camp Verde, at I-17 Exit#285 and AZ 260, go NE 25 miles to US 89A in Cottonwood (and follow the signs to Tuzigoot Monument). Turn left on 89A and go NE 8 miles on Main St. Turn right on FS Rd#999 (to Tuzigoot Mon.). Go across the bridge and immediately turn left on to Sycamore Road-FS Rd#131. Go east 12 miles to the lot and TH.

Hikers refresh themselves at red rock swimming hole on Sycamore Creek.

36 - West Clear Creek Trail FS#17

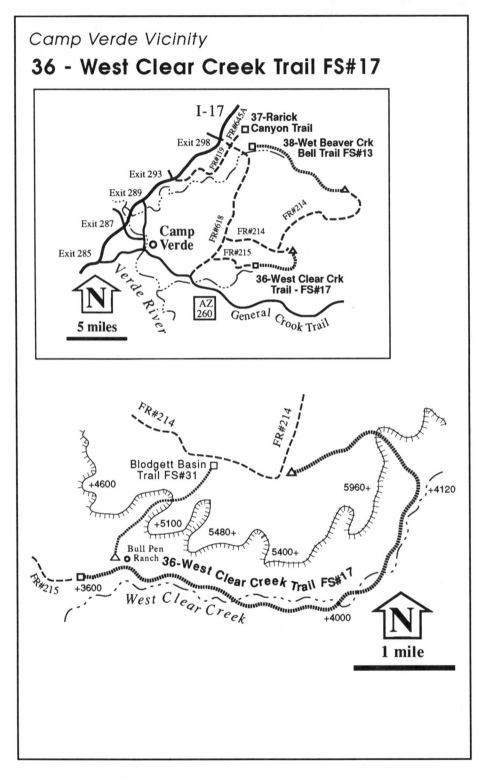

<u>36</u> - West Clear Creek Trail FS#17

* Hot walk for a few miles is rewarded with tree shaded path & swim hole.

Trailhead to Swim Hole
    2.5 mi; 350' gain

Location:	Camp Verde - 13 mi E
Elevation:	3600'
Seasons:	Mar - Oct
Agency:	Coconino NF-Beaver Crk RD
Maps:	Walker Mtn, Buckhorn Mtn

Special: West Clear Creek Wilderness

The United States government was interested in opening the lands of central Arizona. It had been cheaply purchased from Mexico as booty from the Mexican War of 1848. But the rugged terrain and hostile natives had deterred both Spaniards and Mexicans from settling the land for over two centuries. So, the northern portion of the new territory was uncharted and required surveying. To do so, an expedition was organized in 1851 by Capt. Lorenzo Sitgreaves and was led by scout Antoine Leroux. One of the discoveries of this party was the impenetrable canyon carved out by West Clear Creek. It winds its way 60 miles from the Mogollon Rim near Blue Ridge westward to the Verde River near Camp Verde.

Today, this scenic red rock canyon can be accessed at a half-dozen locations along its length, but the easiest is at the west end near Bull Pen Ranch. From the parking area, a trail goes up a hill and around private ranch property, then down to a flat plain near the creek. After a mile-and-a-half of hot, open terrain the trail begins to trace the creek bank and leads to scenic swimming holes at three and four miles. Along the way you'll view Black Mountain to the south and a curious rock cabin covered by a dirt roof with prickly pear cactus sprouting out. It is very hot in the summer, so bring enough water. But the swimming and scenery make the hike well worth while. Lorenzo and Antoine would have agreed.

<u>Directions to Trailhead</u>: **From Camp Verde, at I-17 Exit#285 and AZ 260, go east 8 miles on AZ 260 to MP226.5. Turn left on FS Rd#618 and go north 2 miles. Turn right on FS Rd#215 and go east 3.0 miles to the trailhead.**

Overheated summer trekkers cool off in deep pools along creek.

121

37 - Rarick Canyon Trail

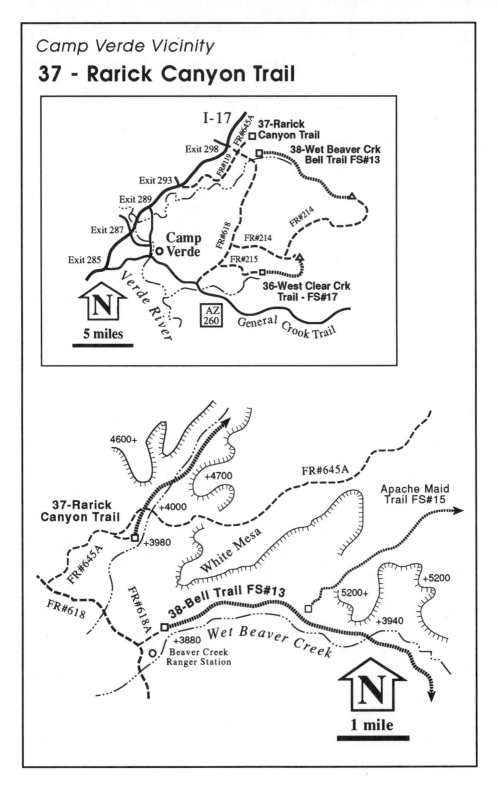

37 - Rarick Canyon

Moderate rock hop by spring stream in lichen-coated red roc[k]

FS Rd#645 to Swim Hole
   0.5 mi; 60' loss
FS Rd#645 to Road Crossing
   1.5 mi; 110' gain

Location: Camp Verde - 16
Elevation: 3920'
Seasons: Mar - May
Agency: Coconino NF-Sedona RD
Maps: Munds Mtn, Buckhorn Mtn

Traditional stream side farms of nomadic Indian tribes were also sites that were much favored by homesteaders. Conflicts arose because the settlers felt they had a legal right to the land while the Indians felt that they had an ancestral right to the land. In 1870, Wales Arnold was the first to homestead Wet Beaver Creek on land by Montezuma Well. Because the area was a natural crossroad, and susceptible to frequent attack by Indians, he didn't build a house, but more of an adobe fort. It proved safe enough, but Arnold's partner, John Burroughs, was attacked and killed by hostiles a few miles away while driving cattle. The ranch was sold by Arnold 10 years later and changed hands many times until repurchased by the National Forest Service in 1947 for development into a national monument.

Rarick Canyon is located a few miles north of Montezuma Well and has a trail that provides a scenic, although rugged, hiking experience for hardy and adventurous trekkers. Less aggressive adventurers can just hike down the creek a quarter mile to a red rock swimming hole or to relax and enjoy a picnic. Or they can travel a half mile further up the lichen-covered red rocks and find ancient petroglyphs inscribed on overhangs that Wales Arnold might have seen a century ago.

Directions to Trail Access: **From Camp Verde, Exit#285 on I-17, go north on I-17 for 13 miles to Exit #298 (Sedona). Turn right on FS Rd#618 and go east 1.5 miles, turn left on FS Rd#645 and go north 1.6 miles. Park the car at a small turnoff labeled FS Rd#9206M and walk down to the creek.**

Trekker trying stone skipping skills at swimming hole in Rarick Canyon.

38 - Wet Beaver Creek - Bell Trail FS#13

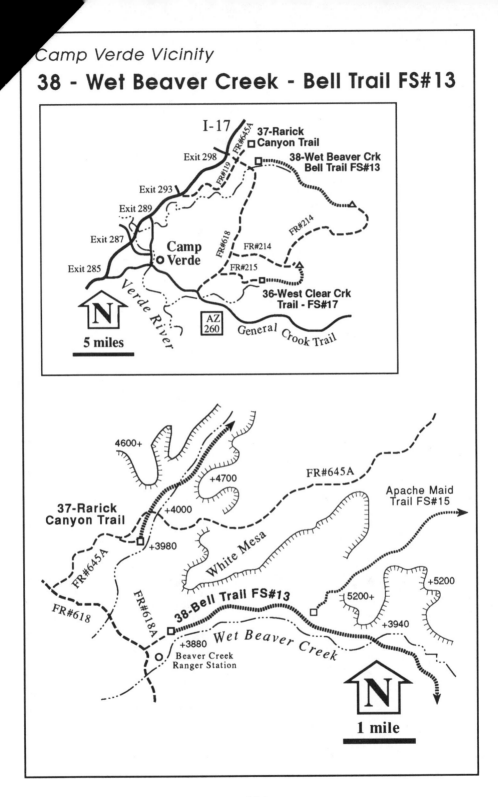

38 - Wet Beaver Creek - Bell Trail FS#13

* Easy walk under cottonwoods next to creek in lush red rock canyon.

TH to Stream Crossing   **Location:** Camp Verde - 17 mi NE
     1.5 mi; 60' gain   **Elevation:** 3880'
TH to Canyon Out   **Seasons:** Mar - Oct
     2.5 mi; 100' gain   **Agency:** Coconino NF-Sedona Dist.
Special:Wet Beaver Crk Wilderness Maps: Casner Butte, Apache Maid Mt

The adventurous and independent life style of the cowboy was much romanticized by novels and silent movies in the early twentieth century. So it became fashionable for wealthy easterners to head west and work the range for a few weeks on a "dude" ranch. Many spreads were located in central Arizona, with one being the Bar D ranch on Red Tank Wash a mile up from Beaver Creek. This was the winter headquarters of the Apache Maid Ranch and was homesteaded in the early 1900s by Benjamin Taylor. Charles Bell, a guest at nearby Soda Springs Ranch, purchased the Bar D in 1932. He upgraded the ranch and built Bell Trail on Beaver Creek for driving cattle to the Rim. He worked and entertained many eastern guests on the ranch, but eventually sold the spread in 1937.

The Bell Trail actually accesses only a few miles of the 22 mile length of Wet Beaver Creek. The first two miles run on an open, exposed trail above the creek in an area covered with prickly pear and agave. The route then intersects the steep Apache Maid Trail which climbs up the north side of the canyon to the Rim. The Bell Trail then descends down to the creek and extends a mile along a well-shaded footpath through the lush red rock canyon. You can stop here, follow the Bell Trail up a steep rocky side canyon on the creek's south side, or continue more treacherously along the creek by wading and walking along the shore.

Directions to Trailhead: From Camp Verde, at Exit#285 on I-17, go north 13 miles to Exit#298 (Sedona), go right on FS Rd#618 and go east 3.1 miles, turn left on FS Rd#618A and go north 0.5 miles to trailhead for Bell #13.

Deep pools are a welcome sight to the overheated summer trekker.

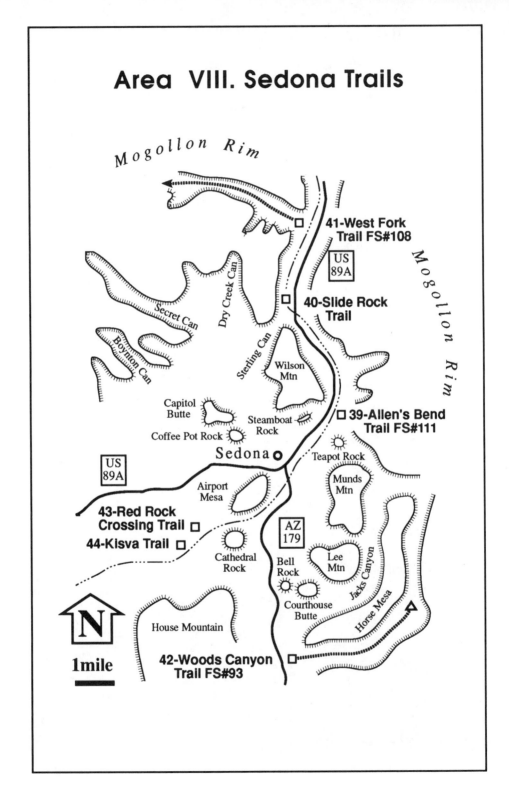

Area VIII. Sedona Trails

Mogollon Rim

Mogollon Rim

41-West Fork Trail FS#108

US 89A

40-Slide Rock Trail

Secret Can

Dry Creek Can

Boynton Can

Sterling Can

Wilson Mtn

Capitol Butte

Steamboat Rock

Coffee Pot Rock

39-Allen's Bend Trail FS#111

Sedona

Teapot Rock

US 89A

Airport Mesa

Munds Mtn

43-Red Rock Crossing Trail

44-Kisva Trail

AZ 179

Cathedral Rock

Bell Rock

Lee Mtn

Jacks Canyon

N

1mile

House Mountain

Courthouse Butte

Horse Mesa

42-Woods Canyon Trail FS#93

Area VIII.
Sedona Vicinity

HIKE DESCRIPTIONS & LOCAL MAPS

39 - Oak Creek - Allens Bend Trail FS#111

40 - Oak Creek - Slide Rock State Park - Creek Trail

41 - West Fork Oak Creek - West Fork Trail FS#108

42 - Dry Beaver Creek - Woods Canyon Trail FS#93

43 - Oak Creek - Red Rock Crossing Trail

44 - Oak Creek - Red Rock State Park - Kisva Trail

Soaring canyon walls dwarf hikers on the West Fork Trail.

39 - Allen's Bend Trail FS#111

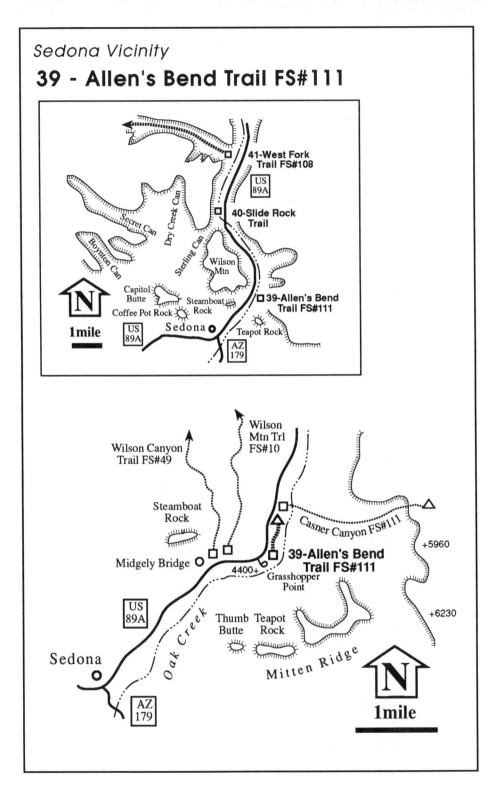

<u>39</u> - Oak Creek - Allen's Bend Trail FS#111

* Cool creekside stroll under a canopy of sycamores & cottonwoods.

Grasshopper Point to Trail End
0.8 mi; 40' gain

Location: Sedona - 3 miles N
Elevation: 4400'
Seasons: May - Oct
Agency: Coconino NF - Sedona RD
Topo map: Munds Park

      Tourism began in Arizona before the territory was even settled. In the 1880s, Prescott miners, Camp Verde soldiers, and Flagstaff lumberjacks pitched tents at the mouth of Oak Creek Canyon and found bountiful hunting and fishing along its length. With time the area's popularity only increased and, in the '30s and '40s, guests were accommodated in lodges and cabins opened on homesteads along Oak Creek. These quarters included a rustic Junipine Lodge built on the old Purtyman homestead which was owned by Charles Allen. The old cabins have since been replaced by a luxury hotel, but the former owner is remembered with his namesake trail.

      Allen's Bend Trail is a short, but scenic route that parallels and skirts Oak Creek. It is one of the easiest and most pleasant creek hikes in Red Rock Country. It is a short and easy stroll on a cool, inviting path along the edge of the floodplain of Oak Creek. There are a few small paths which lead over to the bank (watch out for poison ivy) providing views of water cascading over rocks stacked here and there along the creek. Near the end of the trail you'll discover, illuminated by sunlight pouring through a gap in the trees, a little waterfall above a deep clear pool. Take a lunch break or a swim here and return by the same route.

      <u>**Directions to Trailhead**</u>**: From Sedona, at US 89A and AZ 179, go north 2.4 miles on 89A (MP376.7) and turn right and go down the road that leads to a small lot at Grasshopper Pt. If it is full, which it usually is on weekends, park on the shoulder of 89A. The trailhead is just 75 yards north of the lot.**

Sunlight illuminates Oak Creek cascade and swimming hole along trail.

129

40 - Slide Rock Trail

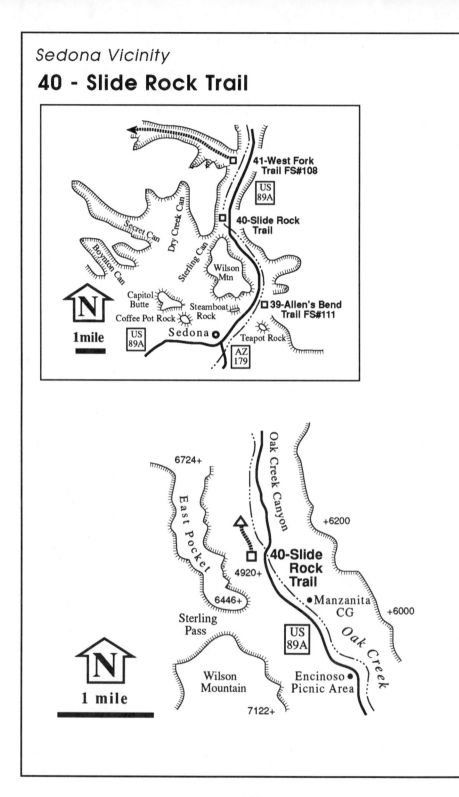

<u>40</u> - Oak Creek - Slide Rock State Park

* Short scenic walk along popular red rock canyon recreation area.

Parking Area to Water Flume
    0.3 mi; 20' gain
Parking Area past Slide Rock
    0.5 mi; 60' gain
Special: Arizona State Park

Location: Sedona - 7 miles N
Elevation: 4920'
Seasons: Mar - Nov
Agency: Coconino NF - Sedona RD
Topo map: Wilson Mountain

Oak Creek's early farmers left a legacy of fine apple orchards that developed a national reputation. One of the most successful homesteaders was Frank Pendley, who left Texas in 1907 and planted an orchard on the grassy meadows above Slide Rock. He reconstructed a little piece of home with a barn that resembled the Alamo. He also built a progressive irrigation system for the 350 apple trees which he had previously watered by hand. In the fall, the apples ripen to a deep red glow that promise a sweet and tangy flavor. You can taste them at the state park store to test their reputation.

There are two options for taking an easy stroll. You can go along a quarter mile trail that is a walk back in time to the orchard and the irrigation flume. Or you can go down to the creek and walk along the red rock slabs past the chutes of Slide Rock. Any time from spring through fall you will see a line of fun seekers skidding through the smooth, slick, water-glazed channels into the very chilly pools of Oak Creek. If you're a photographer, or enjoy a little solitude, you can view the canyon's beauty without the crowds by visiting in colder weather or very early on summer mornings. If you visit in the fall stop in the store, or at one of the road side stands, and try some juice or apples from the orchards.

<u>Directions to the Park</u>: **Starting in Sedona at US 89A and AZ 179, go north 6.8 miles on 89A (MP 381.1) and turn left into the lot. There is a small fee ($3.00 per car in 1993). If the lot is full, you'll have to go much further and park on the shoulder. At the lot, a path takes you down to the creek.**

Kids enjoy the turning and churning of the slippery trip down Slide Rock.

131

41 - West Fork Trail FS#108

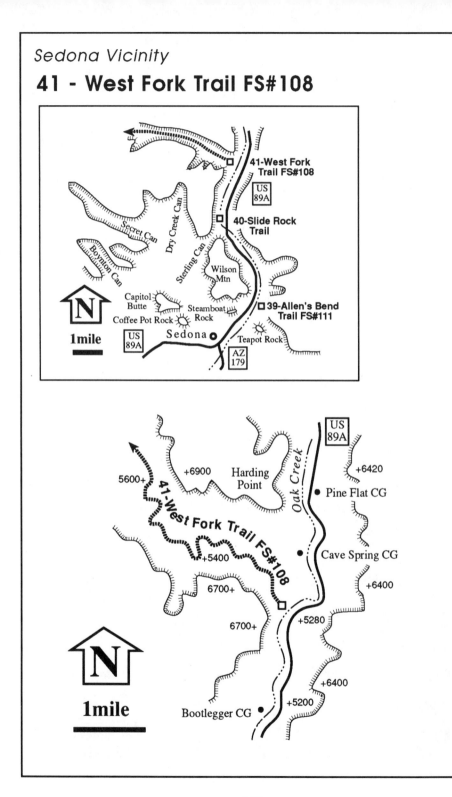

<u>41</u> - Oak Creek - West Fork Trail FS#108

An easy and exhilarating walk through the area's most scenic canyon.

US 89A to Pools
    3.2 mi; 200' gain
US 89A to Rim
    13 mi; 800' gain
Special: Natural Study Area
	Location: Sedona - 10 miles N
	Elevation: 5280'
	Seasons: May - Oct
	Agency: Coconino NF - Sedona RD
	Maps: Munds Pk, Mountainaire
	            Dutton Hill, Wilson Mtn

Some locations in Arizona have such natural appeal that they have attracted characters from pioneer days to the present. Jesse Jefferson "Bear" Howard escaped from California where he had been jailed for accidentally shooting a Mexican sheepherder. In 1879, he became West Fork Canyon's first settler when he built a log cabin at the mouth of the creek. In 1910 Dad Thomas bought the land and developed it into an apple orchard. In 1924, "Call of the Canyon" was filmed there, near the location where Zane Grey had built a cabin and written the story. In the '30s, Frank Mayhew built a lodge that hosted international celebrities, but in the '70s the lodge fell into disrepair and burned down from a transient's fire. The ruins still stand at the canyon's mouth today as a rugged reminder of these colorful characters

The West Fork Trail is an easy trek back and forth across a shallow creek at the floor of a thousand-foot-deep canyon. Verdant green pines, firs, and oaks contrast strikingly against the steep-walled red Schnebly and pale Coconino sandstone. You can stroll up to three miles with little difficulty. It's a good point to stop for a picnic lunch, but if you want to go further, up to 13 miles, be prepared for wading up to your knees or deeper. The best time for hiking is October when the maples and oaks light up the canyon with rich yellows and glowing pinks, but go on a weekday or early on weekends to avoid the crowds.

<u>**Directions to Trailhead**</u>: **Starting from Sedona at US 89A and AZ 179, go 10.1 miles north on 89A (MP 384.4), about 1/2 mile past Don Hoel's cabins, and park on the road side. A driveway on the west side marks the trailhead.**

Red Rock grotto was sculpted over time by erosion from West Fork Creek.

42 - Woods Canyon Trail FS#93

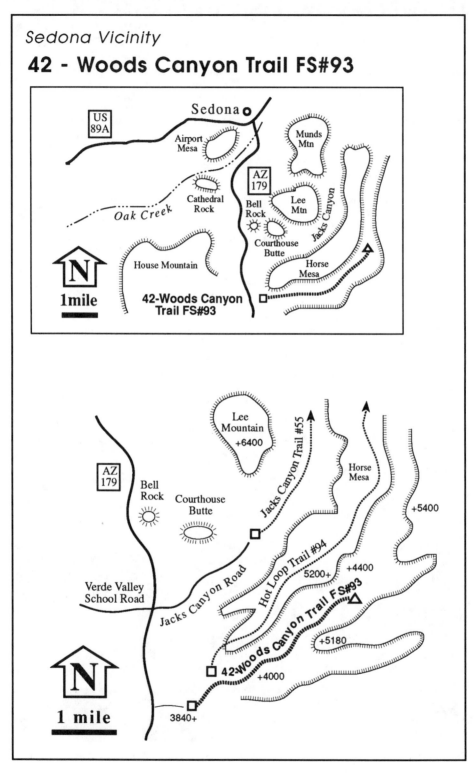

42 - Dry Beaver Creek - Woods Canyon Trail FS#93

* A moderate walk in rolling red rock hills by a dramatic spring time creek.

Trailhead to Trail End
    3.0 mi; 500' gain

Location: Sedona - 9 miles S
Elevation: 3840'
Seasons: Mar - Apr
Agency: Coconino NF-Sedona RD

Special: Munds Mountain Wilderness **Maps:** Sedona, Munds Mtn

Overgrazing of the lush, but fragile grasslands of Arizona in the late 1880s dramatically altered the landscape. Rains ran off the trampled and shaven land too quickly causing wild floods, carving deep gullies, and leaving perennial streams dried out. Grasslands were permanently changed to chaparral and scrub oak. The land only began to recover when, at the turn of the century, the Forest Service reduced the sheep and cattle density by a factor of ten. Before 1900, Dry Beaver Creek flowed 15 miles from the top of the Rim into Oak Creek. Today, it now flows only in the spring during winter snow melt. Woods Canyon is named after a former sheepherder, Fred Woods, who pastured his sheep there in the 1880s.

March is the best time to hike this trail when the winter runoff sends a torrent down the creek. The trail is moderately easy and rolls up and down near the creek bed across relatively exposed terrain that would be hot in the summer. The banks of the creek are lined with Arizona cypress and sycamore which are fed by an underground water flow during summer. The trail dies out after three miles leaving a vista of distant slopes covered with manzanita and pinyon that have replaced the grassy hills which once waved in the wind a century ago.

Directions to Trailhead: **From Sedona, at US 89A and AZ 179, go south 8.3 miles on AZ 179 (between MP 304 and 305). On the east side of the road is a gate with a marker for Woods Canyon FS#93. Drive through the gate and park in about 1 mile. A high clearance vehicle can cross the stream bed, if not flooded, and go about another mile until the road dies out.**

In spring Dry Beaver Creek swells up from winter snow melt.

135

43 -Red Rock Crossing Trail

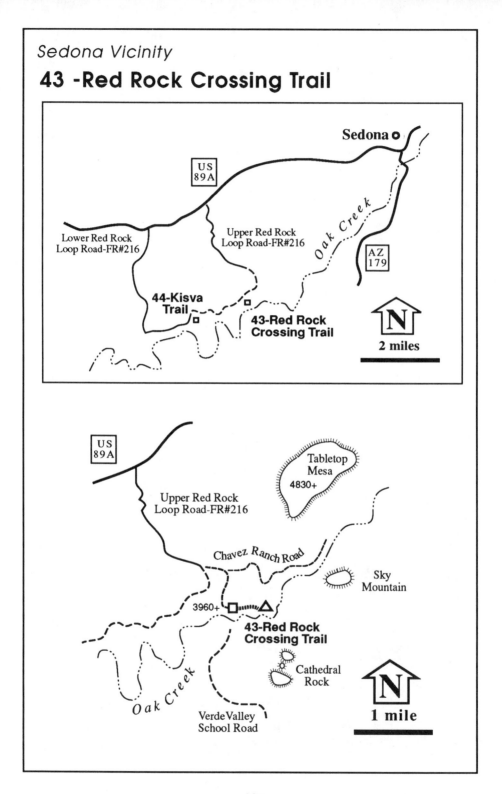

US 89A

Lower Red Rock
Loop Road-FR#216

Upper Red Rock
Loop Road-FR#216

Oak Creek

Sedona o

AZ 179

44-Kisva Trail

43-Red Rock Crossing Trail

N

2 miles

US 89A

Upper Red Rock
Loop Road-FR#216

Tabletop
Mesa
4830+

Chavez Ranch Road

Sky
Mountain

3960+

43-Red Rock Crossing Trail

Oak Creek

Cathedral
Rock

Verde Valley
School Road

N

1 mile

136

43 - Oak Creek - Red Rock Crossing Trail

* Fine views of a classic landmark on an easy stroll by scenic Oak Creek

Parking Area to Boundary
    0.3 mi; 20' gain

Location: Sedona - 9 miles SW
Elevation: 3960'
Seasons: Mar - Nov
Agency: Coconino NF - Sedona RD
Topo map: Sedona

A pioneer's lot in life was one of overcoming adversity, not only of the nature of the elements, but also of the elements of man's nature. In what was one of the Arizona's earliest "land deals", Henry Scheurman bought a 160 acre farm on Oak Creek. The land was purchased in the 1880s, sight unseen, for $500, as a settlement for an old gambling debt. When Henry and his newly wedded wife visited the plot, they didn't find blooming orchards and a sturdy log cabin, but only a wild and untamed area, with a primitive shanty sitting next to an old Indian irrigation ditch. After a year of hard work, Henry harvested his first crop and sold it to loggers and railroad workers in Flagstaff. He then found, discouragingly, that "his" land was actually owned by the Atlantic and Pacific Railroad and was forced to repurchase it, this time from the railroad. But he persevered and prospered until his death in 1926.

Red Rock Crossing is located just south of Scheurman's farm and has a short trail that runs north from the parking lot and the picnic area. The area is most well known for Cathedral Rock's sublime appearance, which changes continuously with the season, the time of day, and the viewing location. Take your camera and capture one of the many moods of Sedona's most photographed landmark, but only visit early or late on the crowded weekends.

<u>**Directions to Trail Access**</u>**: From Sedona, at US 89A and AZ 179, go west 3.8 miles on 89A to Lower Red Rock Road. Turn left and go south 3.8 miles to Chavez Road. Turn left and go 0.8 miles and then turn right on to the road to Red Rock Crossing and park in the lot.**

Cathedral Rock is a favorite Hollywood symbol of the rugged Old West.

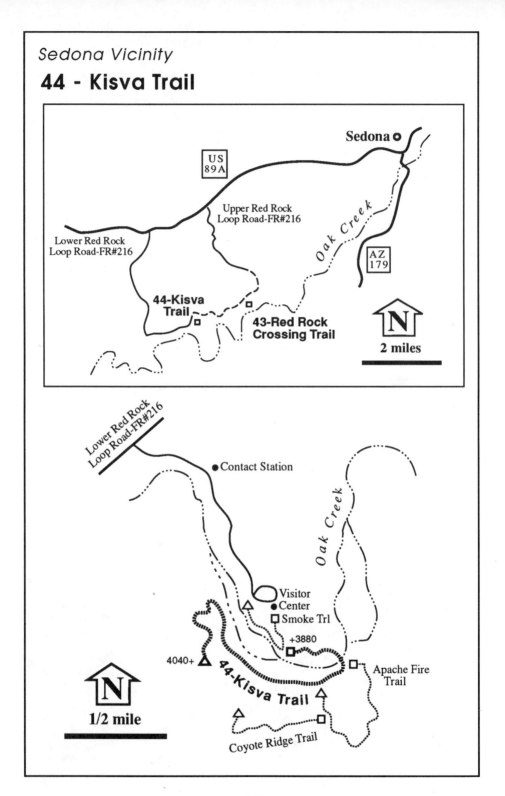

<u>44</u> - Oak Creek - Red Rock State Park - Kisva Trail

A cool, easy stroll by cascades and ripples of Oak Creek.

Visitor Center to Scenic Overlook
1.5 mi; 160' gain

Special: Arizona State Park

Location: Sedona - 7 miles SW
Elevation: 3880'
Seasons: Mar - Nov
Agency: Coconino NF-Sedona RD
Topo map: Sedona

In the early days, before 1900, cattle ranching was a community activity. In the Sedona area, there were more than a dozen ranches with free ranging cattle, that is, they roamed freely without fences. During spring roundup, the ranchers would drive the steers from the valley and the canyons up to the summer range on the Mogollon Rim. After they were brought together, each brand was cut out, calves were branded, and each family's herd was moved to its own area for grazing. A second roundup was held every fall when cattle were driven back down to the valley for winter ranging. One of the ranchers on these drives was Ira Hart who owned a ranch in the late 1890s on the land now occupied by Red Rock State Park.

On the Kisva Trail, or any other of the state park's seven trails, you'll have a chance to experience the terrain and scenery of Hart's ranch. Walk out of the Visitor Center and look at the land. The plains, the hills, and the canyons were all covered with grasses ideally suited for grazing. You can check out the terrain on the Kisva Trail which goes southeast to the bridge, back along the creek, and then up to a scenic overlook. An easier alternative is the pleasant half-mile stroll on the Smoke Trail to the west of the Visitor Center. The trail moves down along the bank of Oak Creek and then back up a short steep slope up to the center.

<u>Directions to Trailhead</u>: **Starting in Sedona, at US 89A and AZ 179, go west five miles on US 89A to Upper Red Rock Road. Turn left and go south two miles to the entrance for Red Rock State Park. Stop and pay the fee ($3.00 in 1993) and go a mile to the center and the trailhead.**

Kisva Trail offers a vista of the new Visitor Center.

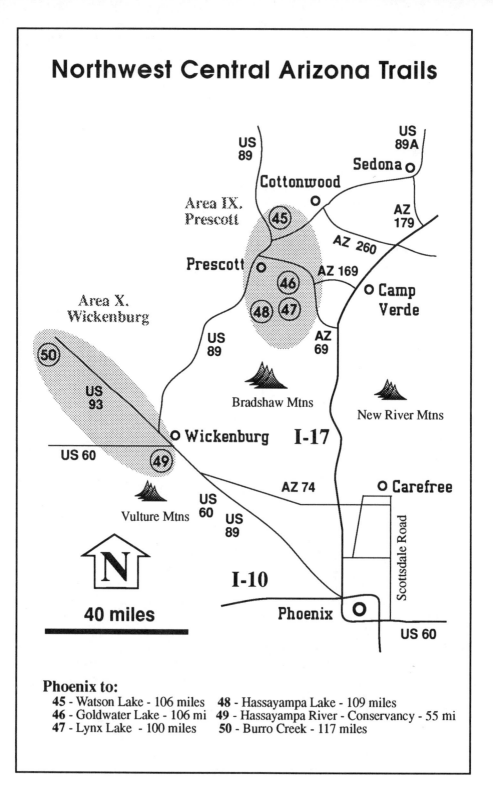

Northwest Central Arizona Trails

US 89

US 89A

Sedona ○

Cottonwood ○

Area IX. Prescott

(45)

AZ 179

AZ 260

Prescott ○

AZ 169

(46)

○ Camp Verde

Area X. Wickenburg

(48) (47)

US 89

AZ 69

(50)

US 93

Bradshaw Mtns

New River Mtns

○ Wickenburg

I-17

US 60

(49)

AZ 74

○ Carefree

Vulture Mtns

US 60

US 89

Scottsdale Road

N

I-10

40 miles

Phoenix ○

US 60

Phoenix to:

45 - Watson Lake - 106 miles   48 - Hassayampa Lake - 109 miles
46 - Goldwater Lake - 106 mi   49 - Hassayampa River - Conservancy - 55 mi
47 - Lynx Lake - 100 miles   50 - Burro Creek - 117 miles

Chapter 7. Northwest Central Arizona Trails

Area IX. Prescott Vicinity

45 - Watson Lake Trail
46 - Goldwater Lake Trail
47 - Lynx Lake Trail
48 - Hassayampa Lake Trail

Area X. Wickenburg Vicinity

49 - Hassayampa River - Nature Conservancy Trail
50 - Burro Creek Trail

Fractured granite blocks surround Watson Lake in Granite Dells area.

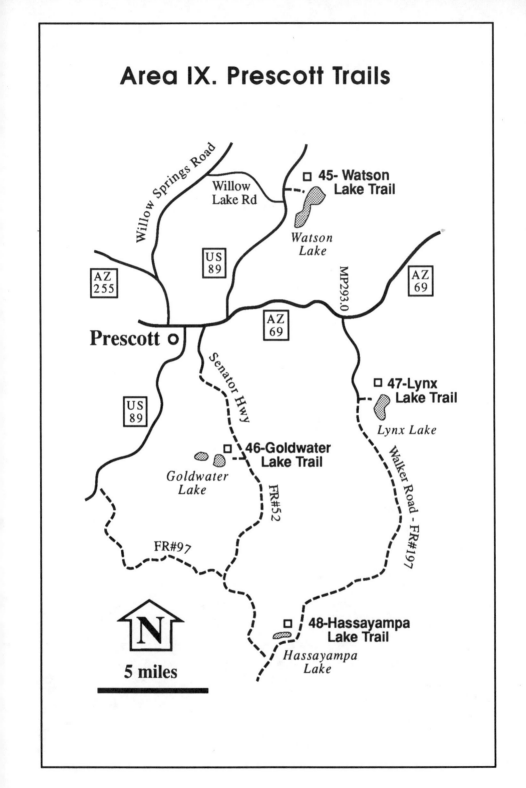

Area IX. Prescott Trails

Willow Springs Road

Willow Lake Rd

□ 45- Watson Lake Trail

Watson Lake

US 89

AZ 255

AZ 69

MP293.0

AZ 69

Prescott ○

Senator Hwy

□ 47-Lynx Lake Trail

Lynx Lake

US 89

□ 46-Goldwater Lake Trail

Goldwater Lake

FR#52

Walker Road - FR#197

FR#97

N

5 miles

□ 48-Hassayampa Lake Trail

Hassayampa Lake

Area IX.
Prescott Vicinity

HIKE DESCRIPTIONS & LOCAL MAPS

45 - Watson Lake Trail

46 - Goldwater Lake Trail

47 - Lynx Lake Trail

48 - Hassayampa Lake Trail

You can always take a hike if the trout aren't biting at Lynx Lake.

45 - Watson Lake Trail

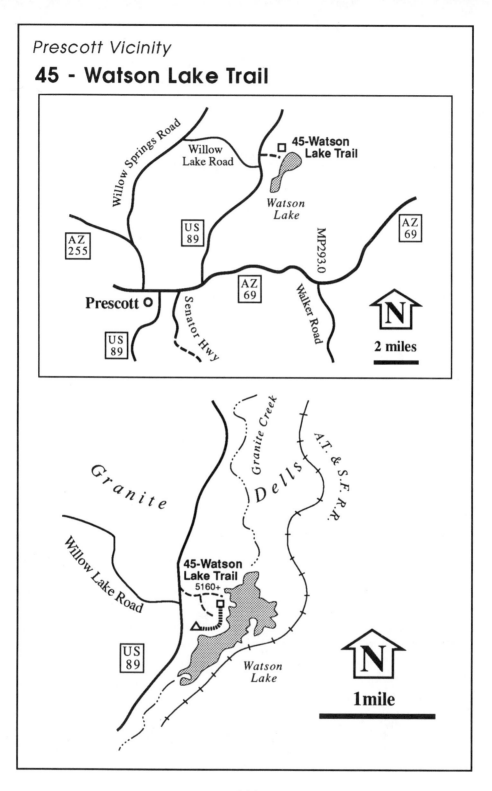

45 - Watson Lake Trail

A rock hop along the granite boulder shore of a scenic lake.

Boat Ramp to Overlook
0.5 mi; 60' gain

Location: Prescott - 8 miles NE
Elevation: 5160'
Seasons: Apr - Oct
Agency: City of Prescott
Topo map: Prescott

Pioneer wives were a tough lot, and bore many of the same hardships and dangers as did their husbands. Louis A. Stevens and his wife homesteaded land near Granite Dells in the early 1880s. Tending the ranch was hard work that sometimes required special duties. On September 20, 1887 Mrs. Stevens sent a note to her husband who was serving at a session of the state legislature in Prescott. The message stated that she was under attack by Indians, and that he should please send ammunition, but that she could hold the ranch. Louis returned home immediately and found his wife and farm animals doing very well.

A visit to Watson Lake will give you a taste of the spectacular scenery that the Stevens' family enjoyed in the Granite Dells area. Although there is no formal hiking trail, there is a fisherman's path with some difficult rock scrambling that can be used to access the shoreline. The huge, jointed granite boulders extend for a couple of miles along Granite Creek. This area has been a favorite recreation spot for almost a century, especially the old Granite Dells Resort and Pavilion that sits a mile down the creek from the lake. Phoenicians visited the resort from the 1920s to the early 1970s when it was closed for refurbishing. It was never reopened. The buildings are now boarded and the pond is empty, but nearby Watson Lake provides a scenic alternative for fishing, swimming, boating, and camping.

Directions to Trail Access: From Prescott, at Montezuma and Gurley, go east 2 miles on Gurley, bear left and go 6 miles north on US 89. Turn right into the Watson Lake CG entrance and go a half mile to the lake.

A kayak glides across calm waters of Watson Lake at Granite Dells.

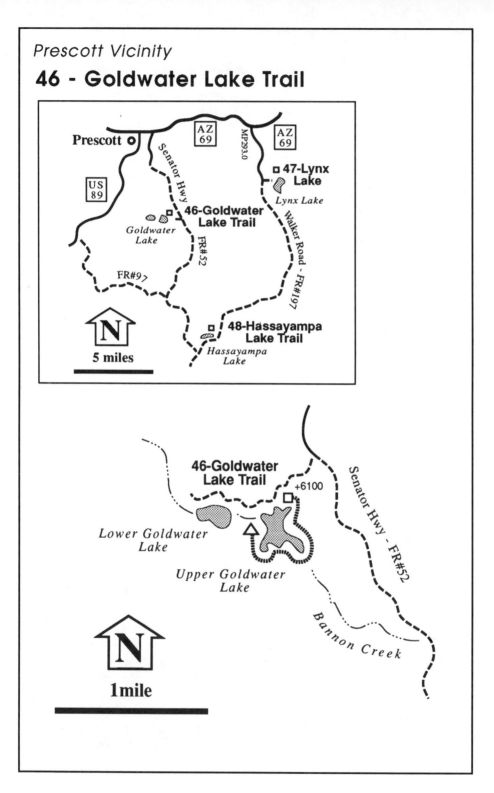

Prescott Vicinity

46 - Goldwater Lake Trail

46 - Goldwater Lake

An easy stroll through a Ponderosa pine forest around an alpine lake.

Picnic Area to Lake Half Loop
1.2 mi; 60' gain

Location: Prescott - 6 miles SE
Elevation: 6000'
Seasons: Apr - Oct
Agency: City of Prescott
Topo map: Groom Creek

Some early Arizona family names still dominate state politics today. The Goldwater brothers, Michel and Joseph, migrated from Austria to America in 1847. They were merchants during the California gold rush but, when the strikes were exhausted, they moved to La Paz, Arizona in 1862. They tried again in Phoenix in 1872, and finally succeeded in 1876 when they established a general store in Prescott across from the county courthouse. Mike's son Morris became active in community affairs and was elected mayor for a total of nine 2-year terms between 1879 and 1927. Morris' nephew learned political lessons well from his uncle and later became Arizona's most famous son, Barry Goldwater.

Goldwater Lake, named after Mayor Morris, was formed in a deep canyon by damming the waters of the Hassayampa River in 1933. The area, dedicated to the citizens of Prescott, is an attractive and well maintained city recreational preserve with picnic ramadas, fishing piers, a hiking trail, but no swimming area. There is a three mile long walking path that traces the edge of the lake next to a pine forest. It follows the gentle contours of the land around the water up to the dam. Since crossing the dam is prohibited, you'll have to turn around there, but you'll see the scenery in a whole new perspective on the return trip.

Directions to Trail Access: Starting in Prescott, at the intersection of Montezuma and Gurley, go east 0.3 miles on Gurley, turn right on Mt Vernon (which goes into Senator Highway) and go south 5 miles, turn right and go west 0.5 miles to parking lot.

Trout fishing skills are tested on piers at the edge of Goldwater Lake.

47 - Lynx Lake Trail

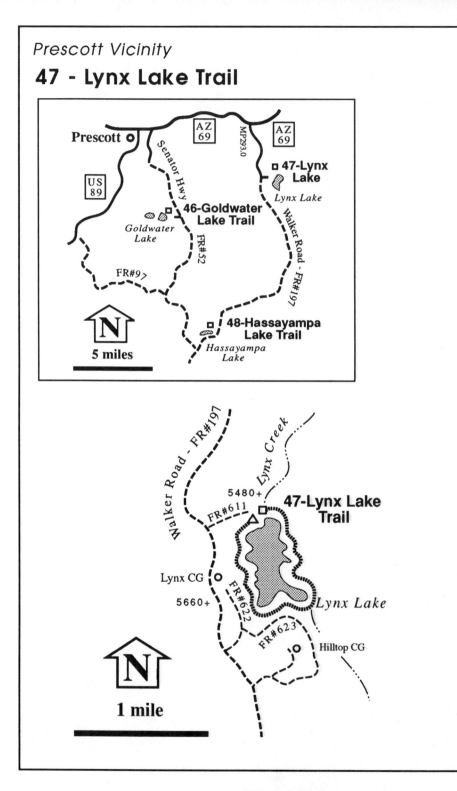

47 - Lynx Lake Trail

* An easy stroll through a Ponderosa pine forest around an alpine lake.

Overlook loop around lake
2.5 mi; 60' gain

Location: Prescott - 10 miles SE
Elevation: 5480'
Seasons: Apr - Oct
Agency: Prescott NF-Bradshaw RD
Topo map: Prescott

Survival on the frontier often caused men to confuse their ethics. The Prescott area was first visited in 1863 by the Walker party. One member, Sam Miller, named Lynx Creek, Arizona's richest stream bed, when an injured lynx bit him as he picked it up. Miller was responsible for the three year Hualapai War because he had shot Chief Wauba Yuma (Big Rump) at a peace conference in 1866. After Miller and brother Jacob became haulers, they moved the territorial legislature from Prescott to Tucson in 1867, back to Prescott in 1878, and finally to Phoenix in 1889. To do this Sam had to keep Jacob from returning to Illinois, so he wrote his brother's wife of Jacob's death and, in turn, told Jacob that his wife divorced him. Sam's colorful, but dubious, character is remembered by his namesake, Miller Valley.

Lynx Lake appears almost as an alpine oasis in a parched and dry land. The mere sight of its azure blue waters and forest lined banks is enough to cool body temperature a few degrees. There is a pleasant, easy 3 mile shore line trail that loops around the lake under the shade of the Ponderosas. The lake is decorated with ducks and geese on weekends and more varied species on weekdays. At the south end is a fishing and picnicking area, while at the north end is a lunch and canoe rental shop. It is a cool spot to spend a midsummer afternoon.

Directions to Trail Access: From Prescott, at Montezuma and Gurley, go east 6.2 miles on Gurley into US 89 east (MP293.0), turn right on Walker Road (FS Rd#197) and go south 3 miles. Turn left on to Lynx Lake Road (FS Rd#611), go 1/2 mile and park at the overlook. Take the path to the lake.

Fishermen test their luck trolling in the alpine setting of Lynx Lake.

149

48 - Hassayampa Lake Trail

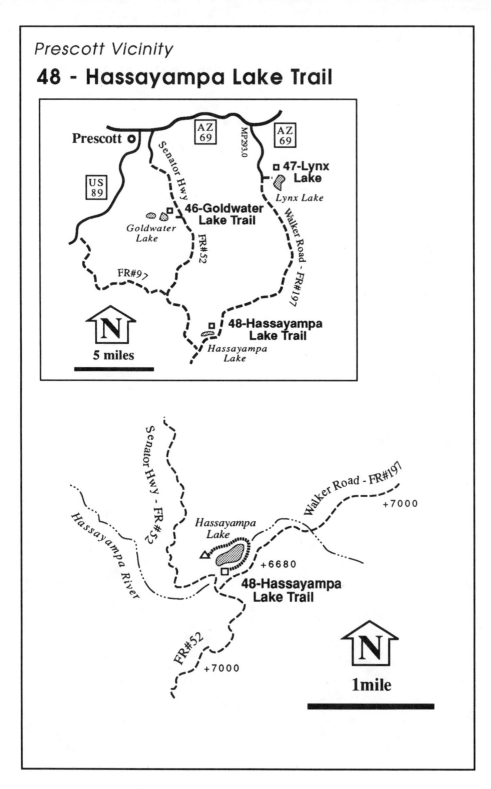

48 - Hassayampa Lake Trail

An easy stroll in a pine and aspen forest by a high altitude lake.

Overlook half loop around lake 0.8 mi; 40' gain	Location:	Prescott - 18 miles SE
	Elevation:	6680'
	Seasons:	Apr - Oct
	Agency:	Prescott NF - Bradshaw RD
	Topo map:	Groom Creek

Gold was Arizona's first lure to pioneers in the late 1850s. Word of nuggets lying on the ground created a boom, even in the hard times of the Civil War. The gold strikes were the basis for the establishment of the territory's first capital at Prescott in 1863. The riches flowing from the ground into government coffers in Washington D.C. helped pay for Union war supplies and was the reason for the Union splitting Arizona off into an independent territory away from the larger block of land of the Confederacy-sympathizing New Mexico Territory. Men flocked to the rich deposits along the Hassayampa and other streams in the Prescott area. Sometimes the value of a claim was exaggerated, but when the truth was discovered, men said drinking from the Hassayampa River made them lie. So a legend developed that said that anyone who drank from that river could never tell the truth again.

The area around Hassayampa Lake is truthfully beautiful. Aspens mingle with oaks and Ponderosa on the the banks of the lake and turn into bursts of gold in the fall. The road to the lake is narrow and winding and there are only a few places to pull off in the vicinity of the bank, but you'll be rewarded with a scenic drive and a quiet destination.

Directions to Trail Access: From Prescott, at Montezuma and Gurley, go east 6.2 miles on Gurley plus US 89 (MP293.0), turn right on Walker Road FS Rd#197 and go south about 12 miles, and park off to the side by a wide part of the road.

Colors of aspen, oak, and maple along the shore are brilliant in the fall.

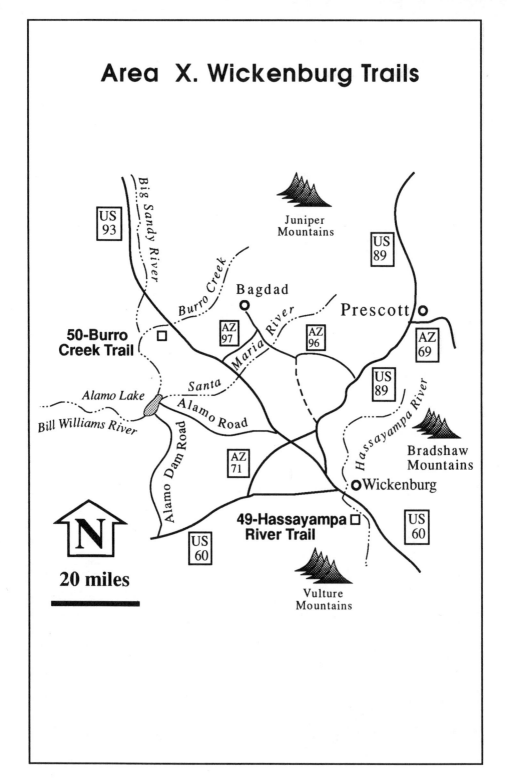

Area X. Wickenburg Trails

US 93

Big Sandy River

Burro Creek

Juniper Mountains

US 89

Bagdad

Prescott

50-Burro Creek Trail

AZ 97

Maria River

AZ 96

AZ 69

US 89

Hassayampa River

Santa

Alamo Lake

Alamo Road

Bill Williams River

Bradshaw Mountains

Alamo Dam Road

AZ 71

Wickenburg

49-Hassayampa River Trail

US 60

N

US 60

20 miles

Vulture Mountains

Area X.
Wickenburg Vicinity

HIKE DESCRIPTIONS & LOCAL MAPS

49 - Hassayampa River - Nature Preserve Trail
50 - Burro Creek Trail

Rich riparian land lies past the graceful bridge that spans Burro Creek.

49 - Hassayampa River Trail

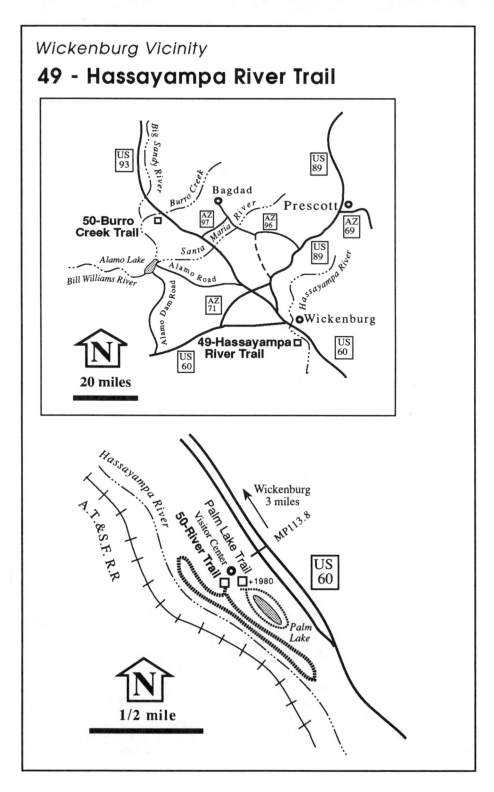

<u>49</u> - Hassayampa Preserve River Trail

An easy stroll along a riparian environment with rich variety of birds.

Nature Center to Trail End
    1.5 mi; 50' gain

Special: Donation suggested

Location: Wickenburg - 3 miles SE
Elevation: 1980'
Seasons: Oct - Apr
Agency: Nature Conservancy
Topo map: Wickenburg

Chance, dumb luck, common sense, or a superstitious sign have all been attributed to the discovery of a new mineral strike. In the fall of 1871 Henry Wickenburg was returning home with a group of prospectors when he saw vultures circling a white, rocky outcropping rising from the desert west of the Hassayampa River. His companions ignored his wish to explore the area, so he returned later and discovered one of the richest strikes in central Arizona, the Vulture Mine. The area eventually produced seven to eight million dollars worth of gold, but Henry had sold his rights to an eastern investment group that swindled most of his royalties.

The Nature Conservancy purchased this plot of former farming and recreational land in 1986 and is now helping it revert back to its natural state. It supports a diversity of wildlife of the vanishing desert riparian habitat and is a favorite stopping place for migrating waterfowl and other itinerant species. There is a half mile trail around the sycamore-lined, spring-fed Palm Lake which has half transformed back into the marsh it once was. You can also take a 1.5 mile stroll along the River Trail at the edge of the Hassayampa River which flows along a broad sandy flood plain. Both trails have nature interest points that highlight the local habitat and species. Walk quietly and talk softly and you just might share a sighting with other binocular-toting bird watchers prospecting for a new discovery.

<u>**Directions to Preserve**</u>**: From Wickenburg, at US 93 and US 60, go SE 3 miles on US 60 to the Hassayampa Preserve at MP 113.8 and park in lot.**

Palm Lake provides a serene setting for a nature walk.

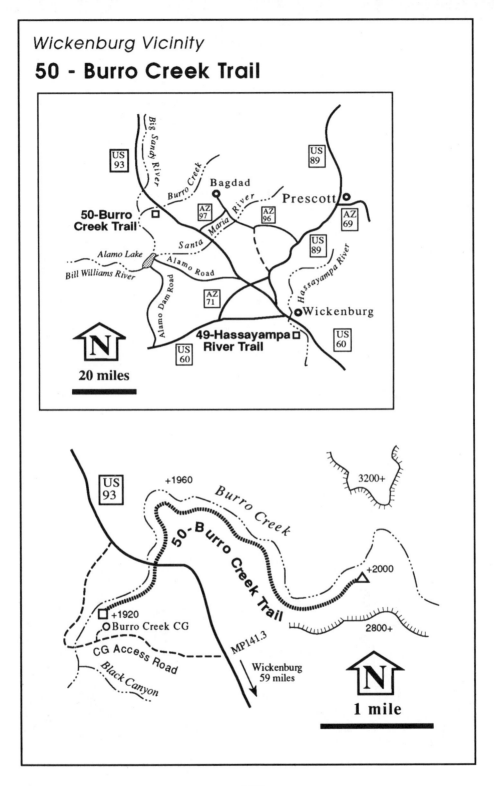

Wickenburg Vicinity
50 - Burro Creek Trail

US 93

Big Sandy River

Burro Creek

Bagdad

50-Burro Creek Trail

AZ 97

Maria River

Prescott

US 89

AZ 96

AZ 69

AZ 71

Santa

Alamo Lake

Alamo Road

Bill Williams River

Alamo Dam Road

US 89

Hassayampa River

Wickenburg

49-Hassayampa River Trail

US 60

US 60

N

20 miles

US 93

+1960

Burro Creek

3200+

50-Burro Creek Trail

+2000

+1920

Burro Creek CG

CG Access Road

Black Canyon

MP141.3

Wickenburg 59 miles

2800+

N

1 mile